LIBERAL UTOPIANISM IS DESTROYING THE UNITED STATES

LIBERAL SECULARISM IS DESTROYING OUR CHRISTIAN VALUES

BY CHARLES KELTZ

Liberal Utopianism is Destroying the United States
Liberal Secularism is Destroying our Christian Values
By Charles Keltz

Printed in the United States of America

ISBN 978-1-61579-035-7

www.xulonpress.com

Acknowledgements:

To my Lord and Savior, Jesus Christ

To Xiao Fang He-Keltz the woman who saved my life

To my nieces and nephews that told me to give it another try

If you like my book you can view my blog at http://www.ck-gentle giant.blogspot.com/?zx=f1bc3222d8cb97c3

CONTENTS

Introduction

This book was written, to show how liberal politicians have tried to create utopia in our country, with big government giveaway programs. This in reality has created a new form of slavery in our society. In a utopian society, no one is in need of anything. That sounds wonderful, but in reality with humans being fallen creatures, this is impossible to achieve. In their attempts to help people, they have managed to make a segment of our society totally dependent on the United States government for their existence.

This book shows a comparison of current events in the United States with the historical records of the Roman Empire and the Chinese Dynasties. There are a few other examples of countries' historical events, in comparison to the United States. This book brings to light, how corruption brought on the financial problems of the Chinese Dynasties and Rome, to where they had to raise taxes, to the point of triggering rebellions and internal strife, which is a prelude for us.

As a history buff, I felt the need to write this book, to warn the people of the United States that liberalism was tried in China 4,000 years ago and it failed. I wanted to warn our society that liberalism has been tried over and over again throughout history, only to fail the society that tried it. I always wondered why people kept trying to enact liberalism into their society. Then it dawned on me that these liberal efforts were an attempt to bring utopia to their society, only to see it fail. Utopia will only come when Jesus returns.

As a Christian, I thought that this book needed to be written to explain that utopia can never be created by Man, because we are fallen beings. This explanation becomes clear in the chapters on the government social programs, which are really giveaway programs that have plunged our society into huge debt. These giveaway social programs have enslaved a segment of our society as illegal drugs have enslaved drug users. I don't know how soon we will see liberalism fail in our country, but I believe we are seeing the beginning of this failure.

While writing about liberals' lack of care for our country, to how their creation of social programs comes first, even if it means the destruction of our country. I have seen almost fifty years of liberal social programs that, in the long run, have created a new form of slavery. Within that process, liberal secularism was born, which has destroyed our moral values. It also occurred to me that liberals can only continue to do this, if we remain uninformed. Examining the liberals' health care ideas, should show you how they care more about their social programs than the welfare of our nation.

I wrote this book in the attempt to get people interested in history. If you study history, you can learn about every nation that rose to world power, only to fall into a meager existence. Every superpower in the past has fallen from some kind of corruption. In our case it will be from liberal secularism.

So why write about liberalism? Why write about how liberals have destroyed the independence of our children, to where they feel they have a right to empower our federal government, to take someone else's property and give it to them? I want to try to wake up the people in the United States before it's too late. I believe we still have time to save our country, but the timeframe is rapidly closing.

I know that it is human nature for people to succeed and to fail. Since a country is made up of people, we can apply this same nature to countries. History can be used to back up this claim. Then you can see for yourself how our history parallels China's history and Rome's history. Then you will understand why the imminent fall of the United States is occurring.

A country's existence is like the existence of a human being. When you are born, you are weak and you need to be taken care of. Then when you advance in life, you become healthy and vibrant, and as you near the end of your life, you show signs of frailty. The

United States is in the third stage of life. We are showing signs of our frailty. It is funny that the average lifespan of a Chinese Dynasty was roughly 268 years, while Rome's lifespan was about a 1,000 years. I believe that our country's lifespan will be closer to the lifespan of the Qing Dynasty.

By studying history, one can see the similarities of one's culture to other cultures, the evolution of religion and the corruption of government politics, which eventually brings on that nation's fall from world power. You can see the rise of Empires and kingdoms; see how they were formed, only to suffer their fall through political corruption. It might even make you wonder how the people of that nation didn't see what was happening to them. Or were they powerless to stop it? I believe they were powerless, because I see how powerless we are to stop our fall from being a world power.

So why write about something you can't stop? So that future generations will at least know that some people, in that time period, cared. To set the record straight on who cared about their country, to who didn't care. To let future historians, who will study the rise and fall of the United States, know how we existed as a nation, in our end of days. This will also let them know that there were a few of us crying out with a plea for us to change course.

The Social Security System

Chapter 1

Liberal Democrats have destroyed our Social Security system. Once again our officials, whom we have elected to go to Washington, D.C., to represent us, have opted themselves out of a system they don't want any part of. Yes, they pay into Social Security, but they don't use it. Or maybe it's better put this way: They don't care about it, because they have other pension plans they can use to support themselves when they retire. Our House of Representatives and our Senators have implemented a retirement plan for themselves, which we pay for, which gives them the cake and has given us the crumbs. One surefire way to save Social Security is to get the decision-making process out of their hands and into our hands, the people of the United States.

Why am I so upset by our politicians opting out of the Social Security system? It's about the same old human nature that everyone has and everyone tries to overcome. Or could it be their breaking of a promise that Social Security will always be there for us? The Social Security trust fund is almost bankrupt.

If you are not involved in the Social Security system, then you won't care about it. If you don't use Social Security, then you won't care what happens to it. It's like someone who doesn't pay any taxes: If you don't pay any tax, then you don't care how high the tax rates go. It also falls under giving people something and expecting them to take care of it, as if they had worked hard to get it. It doesn't happen. That's why I want a committee of private United States citizens to be appointed and come up with viable solution to fix the Social Security system.

We the people of the United States who elect our servants need to regain control of our country. We need to rein in our servants before it's too late. I believe that Franklin Delano Roosevelt is probably turning over in his grave right now. When FDR started the Social Security system, he wanted to get some of the elderly people out of the workforce. By doing so, he felt that this might speed up the recovery of the nation's economy. It didn't work, but since FDR was well liked, they left it in place. It also could have been left in place, so politicians could make it an entitlement program, which in the long haul would give them control over the people, who live in the United States.

Now Social Security is an entitlement program and the politicians in Washington have expanded it, to cover all kinds of disabilities and college tuition for students, who have retired parents. No one wants to give up on Social Security. Everyone expects Social Security it to be there, when they reach retirement age. But since our politicians couldn't leave well enough alone, we have a Social Security system that is rapidly going bankrupt. I wonder why we keep electing politicians that keep expanding government programs. There does come a time, when you have to realize that you should leave well enough alone.

Liberal Democrats now have screwed up the Social Security system, to where it might not be possible to fix it. In other words, get a 401k program started. No, wait a minute; liberal Democrats want to get their hands on that, too. Get an off shore account somewhere, so when you want to retire, you will have some money to live off of.

Why do I say, liberal Democrats have screwed up the Social Security trust fund? FDR was a liberal who started Social Security, and liberal Democrats were in power for over forty years in our House of Representatives and our Senate. Yes, there were brief moments where the conservatives have held power in the Senate or House of Representatives, but when they try to save Social Security, they run into roadblocks from liberal Democrats. It's the liberal

Democrats' way or no way. Here's an example. It is not about Social Security, but it should make my point about what I'm saying about Democrats.

Do you remember in 2001 and in 2003, when George Bush tried to get the Democrats to fix Freddie Mac and Fannie Mae? John McCain tried in 2006. The Democrats said that everything was fine. We all know what happened in 2008. All I can say is: Watch these two YouTube videos. The first one is titled "Shocking Video Unearthed Democrats in Their Own Words Covering up the Fannie Mae, Freddie Mac Scam that caused our Economic Crisis."[1] The second one is titled "Timeline shows Bush, McCain warning Dems of Financial and Housing Crisis: Meltdown."[2]

Liberal Democrats once again have power in Washington, and are they trying to save the Social Security trust fund? If they are, their solution will be to raise taxes. They have no other ideas than that. I don't believe liberal Democrats are trying to save the Social Security trust fund. They are more interested in pork barrel spending disguised as a stimulus package. Out of this stimulus package that was passed into law in 2009, only 9% is earmarked for stimulating our economy; 91% is for pork barrel spending, which will do nothing more than to put our great-grandchildren into debt.

We really need to stop throwing good money after bad. We need to stop electing the same old type of politicians to office, who think big government or raising taxes is the answer to all our problems.

Liberal Democrats did everything they could to undermine conservatives' efforts to save the Social Security system. They use statements, such as this: The conservative Republicans are going to cause the elderly to sleep out on the streets. I didn't see any of this, did you? This didn't happen, and not because liberal Democrats stopped it. In reality, liberal Democrats don't care about the elderly; they are only worried about losing their power.

The federal government programs are not designed to help people; they are designed to make you dependent on government, which gives power to politicians. What's bad is that we the people of this country, bought into the liberal Democrats' spin, and now our Social Security system is in worse shape than when President George Bush tried to fix it.

Liberal Democrats have only used three methods in their efforts to save the Social Security system. One of them was to raise the payroll tax for Social Security, while another was to increase the age of retirement for full benefits. Last but not least, they raised the tax cap on your yearly salary, which is needed to pay up your Social Security for the year. In 2003, any money you earned over $87,000 was free from the Social Security tax. In 2004, it was $88,000. In 1988, my salary was enough to pay up my Social Security tax for that year. Now my salary doesn't even come close.

Our taxes have to be increased every year for the Social Security trust fund because we are killing off our next generation through abortion. "On average, about 3,500 to 3,700 babies are aborted every day," in the United States and we call ourselves a Christian nation. [3]

The next generation always takes care of the generation before them. Lyndon Baines Johnson took $18 billion out of the Social Security trust fund, to fund his great society programs. Then he said the generation of today, which is working, will take care of the ones that are retired. When LBJ said that, it set the stage for all the presidents after him to raid the Social Security trust fund. The last time I checked it, was when George Bush 41 was president, and he took $51 billion out of the Social Security trust fund.

So, do we, the baby boomers, have the necessary people behind us for our retirement? I don't think so. The amount necessary is a six to one ratio, of people working to the one retired. This ratio is to insure our retirement, so we can live out our last days in comfort and allow the next generation to have our jobs. So they can be employed and raise a family. If the numbers aren't there, then that means we will have to work longer, which in turn means we will hold onto our job longer. This means that the next generation will have fewer jobs to choose from.

If you decide to, you can still retire early, but at a percentage reduction, depending on your date of birth. I tell you what, give me the money back that I have put into the Social Security system, and I will guarantee you, that I won't run out of money in eighteen months. Liberal politicians say that you use up all your benefits in this timeframe, but I find that hard to believe.

Let's look at how much money a person from the middle class puts into the Social Security trust fund, and see if liberal Democrats are telling us the truth. If we use a base salary of $50,000 and let's make it simple; you never get an increase in your wages in the 45 years that you're in the workforce. Let's also say liberals never increase the payroll tax for Social Security or increase the retirement age. Now we have the groundwork down – somewhat flawed, though, because you will receive wage increases and liberals will raise your taxes along with increasing the retirement age to receive full benefits.

So the tax collected in one year on your salary is $3,825, and your employer matches this tax, so in one year, Social Security receives $7,650. Multiply that by 45 years and you have $344,250, not counting interest on this money, in the Social Security trust fund. By the way, you only get interest from a bank; government trust funds like Social Security don't pay you any interest, on your money. If you would put this $344,250 into tax-free bonds at 5% interest, you would receive $17,213 in interest per year, and never touch the principal balance. So yes, I think liberal Democrats are lying. What do you think?

Liberal Democrats don't want you to have a say on how your tax dollars get spent. This would get you involved in the decision-making process on your Social Security. They have made sure that you can't take 2% of the payroll tax, out of the Social Security trust fund and divert it to a private fund. I thought liberal Democrats were the party of choice and freedom? They are, as long as you choose to pick the choices and freedoms they give you. Heaven forbid if you choose a different choice and freedom than the ones they have decided for you.

The question the people of the United States need to ask is: What are our servants doing with all this money? I believe that only half the population actually reaches retirement age. So where is the money from these people who paid into the trust fund, but didn't reach retirement age and receive any Social Security benefits? Why do liberal Democrats have so must fear of letting us decide, where 2% of the 15.3% tax we pay for the Social Security system goes? Is it that we will see how poor, of a job, they are doing with our retirement fund? It's estimated that if you start a 401k plan, when you get out of college and just put 3% of your salary into it, without any withdrawals for 45 years. You will have roughly $2 million in that account when you reach retirement age.

So what does this mean? It means that liberal Democrats are lying to us once again. It means that if we wrestled 2% of our taxes back and decided where it should go. Liberal Democrats would have 2% less money, to spend on their worthless social programs.

These federal government programs design by liberal Democrats were designed to enslave people. Liberal Democrats do not want to relinquish control of our retirement fund and give us a chance at it. If the Social Security system was privatized, they would lose the power they hold over us and they don't want that. Another reason is they believe we're too stupid to know what's best for us, so they will decide for us. But I also believe they have done such a poor job that everyone who has an interest in their retirement could run circles around their pathetic efforts.

The Health Care System

Chapter 2

Well, it's time to talk about the health care system, which liberal Democrats in Washington want to force upon us. Two questions have to be asked here. Does a government have the right to force people off a current health care system and onto theirs? Does the same government have the right to force you, to have less protection and raise your taxes to implement their health care system? To me, the answer is "no." What is your answer? Whatever our answers are, we need to contact our elected officials in Washington, D.C., and let them know how we feel about this. Then we will have to let the chips fall where they may.

When Hilary Clinton was given the job to come up with a national health care system, the first thing she did was to break the law, by holding closed hearings. Another way of putting it: She wouldn't allow the current health care providers to attend the meetings, such as insurance companies and the pharmaceutical companies. These types of hearings are supposed to be open to the public.

In the business world, we see what happens when the people with all the knowledge are kept out of the meetings. The meetings run smoothly, but a disaster occurs afterwards. Why is this done? It's done so the people running the meetings don't hear any opposition to their plan or it's done to avoid any tough questions put to them.

So when she was ready to unveil her plan, it was consistent with a typical liberal Democrat plan. Enlarge the United States government and the bureaucratic nightmare that goes with it. Forty new federal government departments would have been created, which would include spending more money than is needed, to provide a viable health care system for the people of the United States. The money was to support the government bureaucracy, not a health care system for the people.

Then she wanted to raise taxes to pay for it and take the freedoms away from the people who already had health care insurance, in an attempt to streamline insurance coverage – if that's possible for the United States government to do.

The United States would have been split up into alliances, which you would have to join. If you chose not to join her system of health care, you would be breaking the law, and you could receive fines or jail time. Most likely they would have been fines, instead of jail time. The money from these fines would have been used to help pay for her health care system.

How is joining an alliance taking away your freedom? By joining said alliance, you couldn't pick your health care or doctor. One other way of saying this is that her health care would be the same as an HMO. In case people don't remember, Ted Kennedy came up with the HMO health insurance system in 1972, to try to stop the rising cost of health care. It failed, as all liberal Democrat attempts do. It seems if you want something to fail, get a liberal Democrat involved.

Now I know what Bill Clinton said in his town hall meetings, and I know what the spin machine was saying, but the fact was that you couldn't choose a doctor. The doctor had to belong to the alliance you were a member of. So why is this so bad? I believe her health care system was based off the HMO's style of health care.

HMOs don't like experimental treatments and refuse to pay for such treatments. Even though Hilary Clinton said these government alliances would allow you these types of treatments, I'm sure you would have to fill out the necessary paperwork, stating why you needed this certain type of treatment.

Do you think that the federal government we live under today would make this paperwork easy, or do you think, as I do, that it would take years before you would get approval from the United

States government? If you don't believe that our federal government would put you through such a monstrous system of paperwork, than you need to look at immigration. Some people have to wait years before they can come to the United States. Just imagine how long this paperwork would take, when it comes to the federal government spending money on us. Probably after a year or two, if you're still alive, you probably would be sent new paperwork to start the process all over again. You would probably need an attorney so you could be treated fairly, and for him/her to stop the United States government's attempt at stalling through the means of bureaucracy.

If you lived in Virginia and were a member of that alliance, and needed to go to Minnesota to the Mayo Clinic for an operation to save your life, the alliance Virginia belonged to wouldn't care, because you're not using up any of their funds, to do so. What you would be doing is using up the funds of the alliance that Minnesota belonged to, and this is where the problem starts. Do you think the alliance Minnesota belonged to would welcome you with open arms, or do you think they might not want you to come? If you do go, their funds for health care would be used on you, instead of their own members. Do you think they would allow this, or do you think they would try to stop you from coming? If you could use the funds of the alliance that Virginia belonged to, do you believe that alliance would allow you to use up their funds, in a location of the country not under their control?

The reason liberal Democrats wanted to come up with a state-run health care system, was to give coverage to the people of the United States, who are not protected by any health care. So instead of creating a health care system for them, the liberal Democrats decided to create a system that would encompass all the people of the United States. Communism is what I call it. Do people have the right to have health care? Yes, if they can afford it. Should the United States government give them health care coverage if they are willing to pay for it? Yes, maybe they should provide it. Providing that the federal government comes up with a system, where these people could get health care at an affordable price. Without shoving the rest of us onto a monstrous federal government, health care system, which a majority of us don't want. One other way of saying this is that the government should give these people health care, at a cost that most people pay, and don't force everyone on to a system, they don't want to belong to.

We already have two health care systems in place, where these people could receive the necessary coverage. One is the Medicare system, the other is the Medicaid system. Why do we need a third health care system that will raise our taxes and achieve the same results as an HMO health care system? I know that these health care systems were created for the elderly and the poor, but all they would have to do is change the charter of one, to include health care for people who have pre-conditions.

Our federal government is the reason for our out-of-control health care costs, due to their Medicare and Medicaid health care systems, along with their high taxes on prescriptions drugs. There is another reason that causes our health care costs to skyrocket, and that is the lawsuits brought against doctors for malpractice. Do we really want our federal government to get involved any further with the health care system we have to live with? My answer is no!

Why write about Hilary's health care when we have a new President, who wants to provide us with a federal government health care system? It really doesn't matter which liberal Democrat is in the office, as our President. They all think alike. Barack Obama's health care system will be the same as Hilary Clinton's health care system. It will be designed to enlarge the United States government, increase the federal government bureaucracy, and be a big money pit, which will do very little for people in need of health care.

Taxation without Representation

Chapter 3

Our country got started by breaking away from England with the excuse of taxation without representation. The tax that England levied upon the colonies, was it as severe as what the Chinese Dynasties levied upon their citizenry? Was it as harsh as our taxes are today, in the United States? No, it wasn't, so what angered the colonists into revolt must have been the lack of allowing them representation in England's Parliament. "In his testimony to the Parliament in Feb. 1766, Ben Franklin estimated the tax rate in Colonial Pennsylvania at 12.5%."[1] If Ben Franklin was arguing for his people over in England about high taxes, what would he be doing now, considering that our tax rate counting hidden tax is 40%?

The statement "no taxation without representation" was the rallying cry that eventually started the revolutionary war, which ended in us obtaining our freedom as a nation. Historians say that during this time in our history, we had 30% who wanted to stay with England and 30% who wanted to break away. There were 40% who just didn't care. Today we have people who want the federal government to take care of them, and there are people who want the federal government off their backs. These percentages of who wants to be taken care of, by the United States government and who doesn't are a little bit different.

The percentages of who doesn't care either way is naturally the remaining percentage of the other two added up. I do know that 42% of the people in the United States feel that the United States government should do more. On a *USA Today/Gallup Poll* on the role of government, as of 3/29/2009, 42% feel the federal government should do more.[2] The same poll shows that the people who want the United States government to do less, and have private individuals and businesses to do more is 50% of our population. Put another way, these people want to make it on their own. The people who don't care either way need to start caring.

Why should these people who don't care either way start caring? People who don't care need to realize that our federal government, which is only 20% efficient, is going to have to raise our taxes to 70% or 80% to have the ability to take care of us. I believe the politicians of the United States government aren't doing this for our benefit, but for their own. So will the people who want to take care of themselves, look upon these tax increases as taxation without representation?

What is taxation without representation? Taxation without representation is where your elected officials ignore what you want; in this case, tax legislation and voting party lines or voting for what they feel is best for themselves. Since our elected officials see the apathy, we the people of the United State have, they are not too worried about being voted out of office. It is interesting to me that some people are willing to give up their freedoms so that they may have theoretical security in their lives. By giving the United States government more control over our lives, we lose the freedoms God meant for us to have, and the freedoms our forefathers fought so hard for us to obtain.

In attempting to have security in their lives and to be kept away from any hardships, some people are willing to give up their freedoms. Why would anyone believe the government of any country could achieve this? I don't know why someone would believe it. What I believe is that these people who want this false sense of security are the people that fall into the 40% category, who don't pay any taxes. These people probably don't care how high taxes go, which means they don't care about their fellow man, either.

Why should someone who wants to mooch off of someone else, care about another person's tax burden? All you would care about is what the federal government can do for you, even if it is at a very inefficient rate, as long as you don't have to pay for it.

Our taxes under our current United States government are higher today than they were when Great Britain had us as colonists. Do I want to be put under the control of Great Britain again? No, what I'm saying is that taxes are in a direct portion to the size of the United States government, which we allow to exist. If we want fewer taxes, then we have to reduce the size of our federal government.

So why haven't we reduced the size of our federal government? That's easy: the people paying the taxes are the minority. Their votes can't sway an election. If their votes could sway an election, then the politicians would pay closer attention to these people's wants and needs. So the people paying the taxes are people without representation in the United States government.

Some people don't know or don't care that 40% of the people living in the United States don't pay any taxes. I know what you are thinking. Yes, they have money taken out of their payroll checks, if they work, as all workers do, but when they do their taxes during tax time, they find out that they get more back than they paid in. These people must think that all of us get this kind of tax welfare, or they must feel that they're entitled to this money. I don't quite understand how someone who doesn't pay any taxes can feel he/she should get a tax cut. This type of thinking is beyond my comprehension. Do I begrudge them another handout? No, I don't. We have welfare programs all through our society; one more will only quicken our fall from world power and give us a larger budget deficit.

What troubles me, are these two situations: One: when I pay $10,500 in taxes and get $3,000 back, which real means I pay $7,500 in taxes. I would like to know why these people who receive a welfare check from the IRS, think, I don't pay my fair share. Two: I don't like our federal government being in the plunder business. I don't think that people in our society have the right to empower our federal government to take from one individual, then give the plunder to another individual that they deem needy.

It seems to me that the middle class gets hit the hardest when it comes to paying taxes. When you make $64,000,000 and you pay $24,000,000 in taxes you still have $40,000,000 left to live on, but when you make $50,000 and pay $7,500 in taxes, you only have $42,500 to live on. There is a big difference here. I don't know how many millions you need to live on but maybe we should be asking Joe Biden, Ted Kennedy or John Kerry. Aren't they the ones screaming that we should be paying higher taxes? I don't know about you, but I have a real hard time living on my salary of $50,000.

Tax Break for the Rich

Why am I willing to let the rich have a tax break and why am I against the redistribution of wealth that liberal Democrats are always screaming for? As long as it's not their money but someone else's money being redistributed? Rich people became rich through hard work. They became rich by investing their money in their ideas, which paid off for them. Some rich people, like Ted Kennedy, inherit it. I wonder if this makes him feel guilty and that is why he is trying to make sure no one else will become rich in the United States.

The rich people who earned their money did it by working hard and taking risks. They invested into the economy and got a return on their investment. When rich people invest into the economy, the economy becomes stimulated, and by stimulating the economy, jobs are created. Giving the rich more money to invest into our economy means a greater chance for our economy to grow and create more jobs. The federal government spending money can't stimulate the economy as efficiently as private individuals can.

Why can't we get the same stimulation of the economy from our federal government? Our federal government is inefficient, so its efforts to stimulate the economy will be 1/5 that of the private sector. Giving the rich a tax cut is bad, according to liberal Democrats. They say the rich should be willing to give more of their hard-earned money to the federal government in taxes. They even call these people unpatriotic, who question these tax increases and feel that they pay enough in taxes. Some rich liberal Democrats say, they shouldn't have gotten a tax cut under George Bush's tax cut policies, but I didn't see any of them giving the money back to the federal government or giving it to the needy.

I will tell you why I think the liberal Democrats have it wrong. It is bad for our federal government to have a $3.5 trillion budget, with a $1.8 trillion deficit, 1/4 of our GNP. The figure that I come up with is by adding our deficit spending to our current federal government budget, which is $5.3 trillion.

$4.24 trillion per year, of the $5.3 trillion of the federal government's budget is wasted. What kind of an economy would we have, if we could use the money our federal government is wasting in a more efficient way? This is why I think the rich should get a tax cut, because I believe they would use the money more efficiently. This would maintain our economy would have fewer fluctuations than any program the United States government could ever come up with. Even if some of the rich decide to give their tax cuts to the poor, it would be done at a more efficient rate than our federal government could ever hope for. Private charities have a 60% to 70% efficiency rate.

Now liberal Democrats will always argue with me and say we should enjoy being the tax base for the federal government. What else would we use their money for? Well, first of all, it's my money, not theirs. What would I use my money for, instead of having the federal government confiscating it? I could make my house payment easer, for one. I could buy a new car, every six years instead of every ten to fifteen years. I could invest it and save it for my retirement. I could give more to charities. There are a lot of things I could do with my money, and be more efficient with it than our federal government could ever hope to be.

I have many questions that liberals don't want to hear or answer, and one of them is: If our federal government is so wasteful with our money, why should we allow them to increase taxes? Why should we give them more of our hard-earned money to start up another federal government program and in the process, take away more of our freedoms? When our federal government wants to control something, they do it through government departments, and through these government departments they set up programs, which never solve any problems. They just control and regulate them. Why's that? Because that would mean if they did solve a problem, they would have to close that government department. So our federal government doesn't solve problems, it regulates them. This keeps the federal government growing, which in turn increases its workforce, and by increasing its workforce, it will need more of our money.

If we allow our federal government to increase our taxes as liberal Democrats want. Then in the process of them increasing taxes, they will enlarge government, which will in turn, intrude more into our everyday lives. Larger governments always mean more government control, which means more freedoms taken away. We the people of the United States need to start asking ourselves this question: How much government should we allow into our lives? The larger the federal government gets, the more taxes it will need to confiscate, to run said government.

Has anyone read the tax poem that is on the internet, which gives all the taxes that have been created in the last 100 years? It does state that not one of these taxes existed 100 years ago, but I believe if you look into it, you will find that most of these taxes didn't exist 50 years ago. Liberal Democrats didn't get the nickname "Tax and spend" for nothing. Here's a list of the taxes spelled out in the web site Tax Poem.

Accounts Receivable Tax, Building Permit Tax, CDL License Tax, Cigarette Tax, Corporate Income Tax, Dog License Tax, Excise Taxes, Federal Income Tax, Federal Unemployment Tax (FUTA), Fishing License Tax, Food License Tax, Fuel Permit Tax, Gasoline Tax (42 cents per gallon), Gross Receipts Tax, Hunting License Tax, Inheritance Tax, Inventory Tax, IRS Interest Charges, IRS Penalties (tax on top of tax), Liquor Tax, Luxury Taxes, Marriage License Tax, Medicare Tax, Personal Property Tax, Property Tax, Real Estate Tax, Service Charge Tax, Social Security Tax, Road Usage Tax, Sales Tax, Recreational Vehicle Tax, School Tax, State Income Tax, State Unemployment Tax (SUTA), Telephone Federal Excise Tax, Telephone Federal Universal Service Fee Tax, State and Local Surcharge Taxes, Telephone Minimum Usage Surcharge Tax, Telephone Recurring and Non-recurring Charges Tax, Telephone State and Local Tax, Telephone Usage Charge Tax, Utility Taxes, Vehicle License Registration Tax, Vehicle Sales Tax, Watercraft

Registration Tax, Well Permit Tax and Workers Compensation Tax.[3]

"Still think this is funny?"[4] How many of you think we should be paying these taxes? How many of you think that we are undertaxed? I don't mind paying some of these taxes, providing that the money collected is only used, for the tax in the title. For instance, one of these telephone taxes was created to give internet access to school children. I don't want to pay that tax. Quit disguising these taxes and spell them out in an accurate way so we know what we are being taxed for.

A New Form of Slavery

Chapter 4

The liberal Democrats have created a new form of slavery, which has existed in the United States for over forty years. This slavery started back in 1964, under Lyndon Baines Johnson's Presidency. President Johnson came up with legislation he code-named the Great Society. Not all of his legislation was bad, just the parts that promoted single parenting, illegitimacy, abortion, and the parts that put people under the control of the United States government.

The parts of his legislation that were good for the United States were the elimination of discrimination based on race. "It authorized the Justice Department to bring suit against states that discriminated against women and minorities" and the part of his legislation that "guaranteed equal opportunities in the work place."[1] It would have been nice if they would have stopped there, but they didn't. It seems that our society doesn't know when to leave well enough alone.

Now let's discuss the parts of his legislation that have devastated the family's structure, bringing on single parenting and illegitimacy, which have destroy the moral fiber of the United States. The Great Society was created under the masquerade of caring for the poor and elderly.

What it did in reality was to make a certain segment of our society totally dependent on the United States government for their existence, which in this deception secured a voting base for the liberals in Washington. Being totally dependent on our federal government is a form of slavery because it puts you under their control. You live and breathe with the hopes that they will continue to take care of you, instead of you standing on your own two feet and taking care of yourself. When you are dependent on someone or some organization, you usually do what they tell you to do, or maybe it should be put this way: Being dependent on someone or some organization, with nothing to fall back on, such as a career or an education, makes you think twice before you vote against the people feeding you.

Our House of Representatives and members of the Senate of our federal government made modifications to welfare in 1988 and in 1996. I believe some of the modifications done in 1996 had corrected some of the problems, but didn't solve all of them. Now that Barack Obama has been elected as our president, he has, through executive order, repealed these changes and has turned back the progress made on welfare reform.

What our representatives should have done in 1964 was to find a way to keep the family together with financial aid. This would have allowed the husband and wife to improve their status through job training or an education. What our representatives in our federal government did do, in 1964 with welfare, was to create an illegitimacy problem that has never existed in recorded history. One of the ethnic groups in our country at one point in time had a 70% illegitimacy rate. Where did I get this information? I heard it on the Bill O'Reilly TV News hour, and he got his information from the Census Bureau.

The Illegitimacy Rate

The illegitimacy rate for Black babies in the 1960s was 22% before welfare started; it is now 68%, down 2% from its high of 70%. The illegitimacy rate for Caucasian babies in 1956 was 1.9%. In 1990, the illegitimacy rate for Caucasians was 17%, and in 2002 it was 23%. "Although Hispanics are widely considered morally traditionalist, their illegitimacy rate is almost midway between the white and black rates."[2] The Hispanics illegitimacy rate is 43%. It's interesting about all these illegitimacy rates. In the "Northeast, Asians have the lowest illegitimacy rate among Americans, with both Chinese and Japanese being under" 10% in 2000. [3]

I believe the illegitimacy rates in our country are a direct result of welfare. I also believe that the high crime rates in these communities are a direct result of welfare. One must ask if receiving welfare from our federal government, which is just enough to keep you alive, promotes crime.

When rich people have nothing to do with their free time, they set up help organizations. What do poor people do when they have nothing to do? What they do with their free time is spent out on the street, and their role models in these communities are drug dealers, pimps, prostitutes and drunks. These are not the role models I would want my children to have. How about you?

If these people living in these communities are waiting on our federal government to pull them out of poverty, then they are going to have a long wait. They have already waited for 40-some years. I would think they would be getting tired of waiting.

If the United States government wanted to help the poor, then why did they set up a system that reduced the welfare benefits to the family, as non-welfare income increased? In reality, what it did was create single parenting. The welfare system would only render maximum support to a family as long as the father was gone. Why didn't they set up a system that would help pay the bills of the poor family, while they put the father through college or a skilled trade school, which in turn would have made him a better provider for his family? This would have given the father some self-worth. Instead our representatives in our United States government decided to put the federal government in charge and replace the father. I think the United States government is a poor role model as a father for our children. What do you think?

So if you want maximum aid from the federal government, the father of the family will have to leave – in other words, be an absentee dad. They also set up the system that for each additional child the woman had, she would receive more money. Isn't that an incentive to increase the illegitimacy rate? Plus, doesn't this make sure that these people on welfare stay on welfare? They put on the noose of slavery called welfare, and they don't even know it.

Is welfare the only cause of illegitimacy in our society? Probably not, but I believe that this type of welfare our federal government set up caused a snowball effect. You do have to ask this question: If welfare didn't cause the illegitimacy rate to go up, then what did?

How has welfare caused this? Welfare doesn't exclude aid to married couples. What welfare does is penalize marriage through the means-tested programs. The means-tested programs supply aid and benefits to families. These benefits get reduced as non-welfare earnings increase. The means-tested programs supply food, housing, cash, medical care and other services to people in poverty.

"Between 1965 and 2000 welfare spending cost taxpayers $8.29 trillion (in constant 2000 dollars)." [4] You would think that with this kind of money being spent on welfare would eventually pull these people out of poverty. What's interesting here is welfare spending goes up every year. It's not that money is being held back from these programs. So why hasn't welfare pulled these people out of poverty?

Welfare that helps people in poverty with medical insurance, food and housing should be a welcome relief to people in this situation, but as with all federal government programs, there is a catch. You have to break up your family to get the maximum amount of aid and be totally dependent on the federal government for your existence, which is not living. I believe this is why some of these people become so angry. They see other people going out having fun while they are stuck at home with just enough welfare aid for them to exist. As you will see by reading further, the aid you receive is not much in the way of help, but it's better than minimum wage.

"The poverty thresholds are the original version of the federal poverty measure."[5] "They are updated each year by the Census Bureau."[6] So what is poverty? The United States government describes poverty in regards to income. "Poverty guidelines issued from 1965 to 1982 had separate figures for farm and nonfarm families."[7] The poverty line in December of 1965 for a nonfarm family of four was $3,130 per year. Minimum wage was a $1.25 per hour, which comes to $2,600 per year. As of 2009, the latest information I could find shows the poverty line for a family of four to be $22,050 per year. This amount is in the continental United States. In Alaska the poverty line is $27,570 per year, and in Hawaii it is $25,360 per year. Minimum wage in 2009 is $7.25 an hour, which comes to $15,080 per year.

These figures are from 2002 when I lived in Northern Virginia, since I know how much it cost to live there. So let's look at a single mother living in Northern Virginia. So what dollar amount did a welfare recipient receive in aid and benefits back then? Her monthly cash amount with food stamps was roughly $389. The rent for an apartment in Northern Virginia was anywhere from $800 to $1,500 per month. She is also entitled to energy assistance, which we will average to $100 per month. So how much does this come to, on a yearly base? Let's see, if we take the average monthly rent and add all this up, it comes to $19,668 per year without counting Medicaid. So let say with Medicaid, we'll round it to $20,000 per year in aid and benefits. Minimum wage in 2002 was $5.15 per hour. So if you can get welfare at $20,000 per year, why would anyone want to work a job at minimum wage, which came to $10,712 per year?

I didn't see any minimum wage jobs in Northern Virginia. What I saw was starting wages at companies, which would normally pay minimum wage at $7.50 per hour, which is $15,600 per year. So it's still better to be on welfare than to have a job with one of these companies. This, to me, is some evidence to show that once you're on welfare, you are going to stay on welfare. What is the incentive to get off welfare, if you can get $9,000 more a year instead of working at a minimum wage job? You can stay at home and basically do nothing. This is a problem all to its own. Staying at home becomes very boring.

Now, if a single mother on welfare meets a single man who is working, why would she want to get married to him? Her benefits, as soon as they got married, would be reduced or completely eliminated, because as non-welfare money increases in the family, welfare money gets reduced. So this man, who is working has a job that pays $20,000 per year, but instead of them having a combined income of $40,000 per year, they would have to live on his salary of $20,000 per year. You can't make it in Northern Virginia on $20,000 per year. So what they do is stay unmarried, so she doesn't lose welfare benefits.

The United States government's refusal to help needy families in a productive way, back in 1964 by not allowing them to keep welfare money, while the man of the house was working. This is a direct cause, of the rise of the illegitimacy rate in these families, on welfare. By this process of our federal government's attempts to take away welfare money as non-welfare increased, was a direct result of single parenting. The woman on welfare, who doesn't want to lose her aid will stay single and probably will just live with the man of her choice. It seems that welfare replaced the husband, but did nothing to secure guidance and discipline in the family that the father would have provided.

So why am I blaming LBJ for the mess that we're in today? The Great Society was a modification to or an addition to the Social Security Act of 1935. The food stamp program was enacted in 1964, which increased the potential for people, to be totally dependent on the United States government for their existence, instead of finding a way to get them to earn a decent salary, which would allow them to stand on their own two feet.

The Social Security Act of 1935, under Franklin Delano Roosevelt's presidency, is what started welfare as we know it today. Yes, it is true, the Social Security Act of 1935 brought in old age benefits (retirement benefits), unemployment, and aid to dependent children, just to mention a few. The aid to dependent children of the Social Security Act of 1935 was usually for women who were widows, but there were exceptions. This enabled the women to stay at home and raise their children. Today, the money for aid to families with dependent children seems to go to single women who have illegitimate children.

Why hasn't aid to families with dependent children helped these families? It hasn't helped because it breaks up the family, instead of strengthening it. The families that were in poverty or in need of assistance didn't get much help if the father was earning a salary and lived at home. So the fathers of some needy families, who wanted the maximum amount of aid for the family, would swallow their pride and leave their homes. This allowed the women to get the maximum amount of welfare aid.

The Great Society Legislation

The Great Society legislation was passed by the 89th Congress, which enacted massive federal government spending on social programs. One of these legislations was named AFDC (Aid to Families with Dependent Children). AFDC is the most recognized identifier of welfare. It allowed women to receive government aid to raise their children, if they met the requirements for such aid.

Has LBJ's Great Society helped these people? I don't believe it has. In his attempt to help these people, he wanted to improve the inner cities. So, has welfare helped, to improve the inner cities over the last forty years or so? If anything, I believe it has made things worse. It has made a lot of people think that Black people can't make it on their own, even though there are more Caucasian people on welfare than Black people.

When government departments are formed, they never fix the problems they were designed to fix. What these United States government departments do is regulate the problem. If government departments ever fixed the problems they were created to fix, they would have to close down or be seriously reduced in manpower and size. Since liberal Democrats don't want their god to be reduced in size or power, they will do everything they can to make sure the federal government is increased in size and power. This is why liberal Democrats love to increase our tax burden and why our taxes are 40% of our salaries. Hidden taxes are calculated into this figure.

What we should be asking ourselves is this: If the government departments only regulate problems such as crime, drug dealing and poverty, has anyone ever been helped by these programs? I believe we know the true answer: They have not. So by 2009, we have wasted over $9 trillion of taxpayer money. So what should have been done with this money?

How about going into these cities and setting up training and work zones? The local people of the inner cities, who want to learn the building trades and those who want to open a business could have gotten some form of government aid, to do so. We could have brought in the necessary resources to get things started. We could have torn down all the old building and built new ones. This would give the opportunity to the local people to learn the building trades.

The people who want to start a business could have their building built, while learning how to run their business.

Yes, I know if we were to start this, they would have to be protected from gang members and criminals. This means law enforcement teams that can be trusted, would have to watch over them. I believe if you get the people from the local communities to rebuild their cities, they will take pride in their workmanship as well as their cities.

We the people of the United States need to ask ourselves another question: Do we want a big federal government to take care of us and to get bigger in the process, or are we going to start accepting responsibility for our actions, and benefit or suffer from the decisions we make in our lives? One thing is for sure: Big government is only going to make things worse. If we continue down the path of allowing our government to get bigger and be more intrusive in our lives, we will be paying 60% of our wages in taxes in a very short period of time.

As asked above: Has the United States government helped the inner cities? I believe this will speak for itself. For instance, how many people who could afford it, have moved out of the inner cities? How many people today in our society want to move into the inner cities? Of the people who managed to move out of the inner cities, how many want to move back or are they glad they're out? These people who move away from the inner cities, moved to the suburbs, away from the violence and crime. The inner cities that LBJ wanted to make a better place to live are worse off today than before the Great Society was started.

Why are these cities worse off today than before the Great Society? Being on welfare programs doesn't pull you out of poverty it just gives you enough to survive, with no hope to improve yourself. It also gives you a lot of free time. In having this free time, what do you think these people do? A lot of them turn to crime, some join gangs, while others will play sports. The only harm that occurs with someone who plays sports is the lack of an education. So if they don't make it in sports, they will have to take a low-income job or go on welfare. The ones who join gangs usually try to intimidate law-abiding citizens, to give them money. They will mug people and do other criminal actives such as stealing cars, robbing stores, drug dealing and probably prostitution.

Has the education of the poor improved? No, it hasn't. If anything, the quota system (Affirmative Action) has hindered the education of the poor. Why is this? Affirmative Action guaranteed that a certain portion of the minorities receives a spot on the school rosters. How is this bad? When you know that you have a guaranteed spot for a college, you don't have to apply yourself in school. This is why you have seen some scores of the minorities in the lower half of the test score for college admittance.

Charity is not the Job of Our Federal Government

Charity is not the job of the United States government, but the job of charitable organizations. These charities were created by religious organizations or people, who wanted to take care of the needs of the poor. In a charitable organization, you can give or you can choose not to give. You have the right in a free society to give or not to give. Therefore, no one has the right to force you to give. This is why our federal government should not be in the charitable business, they force people to give through taxation.

Slave Reparations

Chapter 5

What are slave reparations? Slave reparations are the attempt to get someone to pay for the discrimination done to a certain people, 140 years ago. Why should we do this? Some people feel it will stop racial tensions. Some people feel guilty for what their ancestors have done to these people.

Will this stop the racial tensions in the United States? No, probably not. If anything, it will intensify them. Innocent people don't like paying for something they had nothing to do with. I also believe that a large segment of our society is getting tired of hearing about how bad some people had it and have it. When most of us are working one full-time job with a part-time job to make ends meet. It is time we get over it and get on with our lives.

What about the people who feel guilty for what their ancestors did? If it makes them feel better about themselves, then they can set up a trust fund for these people and they can pay into it. If it helps them to get closure for what their ancestors did, then more power to them, but I don't think that these people who want closure over the deeds of their ancestors, will be satisfied with a trust fund. They want to empower the federal government of the United States to confiscate innocent people's money and then give that money to the victims of their ancestors. I'm totally against such actions.

Why am I against this? Slavery was legal back then. Yes, you can argue that slavery was morally unjust, a crime against humanity, and

I buy all of it. But we have immoral laws on the books today. One of these laws is abortion. Another reason I'm against slave reparations is because innocent people would have to pay for said reparations, through higher taxes. Forcing innocent people to pay for something they didn't do is an immoral act unto itself, and probably just as bad as slavery. Who are these innocent people? Anyone that is living in the United States today that pays taxes. If children are not held accountable for their parent's actions, how can we hold them responsible for their grandparent's or great-grandparent's actions?

I know some people are trying to say that back in the 1860s, you were either a slave or a slave owner, but they are wrong. There were people in the United States who weren't slaves or slave owners. They were the working class; people who were just trying to survive and make ends meet. Should we force slave reparations on the children who had grandparents or great-grandparents who were slave owners? No, once again we have laws in place that say children cannot be held accountable for their parents' actions.

To get around this law, people who are for slave reparations are trying to hold the federal government accountable for this immoral act, but who does the federal government represent? They represent the people of the United States. Can our federal government of the United States be held accountable for past actions against a people, who are no longer living? I say no, the federal government is made up of people who live in this country, and back then, the majority of Southern White people wanted slavery.

When Should Slave Reparations have been attempted?

Slave reparations should have been attempted right after the Civil War or soon after Abraham Lincoln freed them. I know what some people will say, and I realize that the Civil War was not fought over slavery, but that war freed the slaves indirectly. The Emancipation Proclamation was issued back in 1863 by Abraham Lincoln, which freed all slaves, in states, which were in rebellion against the federal government of the United States. I know that this did nothing for the slaves, in the states, which were still a part of the United States, and it surely didn't free the slaves in the states that were in rebellion, but it started the ball rolling, and in 1865 all slaves were supposedly freed.

Why do I say that slave reparations should have been attempted back then? The people who were discriminated against were still alive; the wrong done to these people had a better chance of being righted. These people could have brought a lawsuit against the federal government, to the Supreme Court of the United States, asking for damages. Do I think they would have gotten anything for the wrong done to them? No, but they could have kept at it and maybe somewhere down the road, say 20 years or 30 years after the Civil War, they might have gotten some justice.

The Japanese Americans who survived our holding camps brought a lawsuit against the United States, 40 years after WWII, and received compensation for land taken away from them during WWII. Their compensation was set at the value of the land at 1945 prices. How is this different from slave reparations? The taking away of land from these Americans was illegal. There has been another case involving the illegal taking of land from the Sioux Indians. The Sioux Indians brought the case to the Supreme Court of the United States and won their case in 1980. They received a cash settlement, which they rejected. They want the Black Hills of South Dakota back; they probably won't get it, but that's what they want.

Should Slave Reparations be paid to the Jews by the Iraqis, Egyptians and Persians?

Should slave reparations be paid to the Jews by the Iraqis, Egyptians and Persians? The Babylonians, the Persians and the Egyptians had the Jews as slaves somewhere in their histories. If time does matter, and we think that children should be held accountable for their ancestors' actions, then by all means the Jews are entitled to compensation.

If we are going to hold the Iraqis, the Egyptians and the Persians responsible, then we need to hold the Italians responsible for having slaves, too. The Roman Empire took slaves from the land they conquered. We mustn't forget about the English, either; they had slaves also. If you realize what I'm trying to say here, that's good, but for the people who don't understand: If we were to look back into our heritage or family trees, we probably could find that one of our family members or relatives was a slave, which would make us entitled to slave reparations.

So who should be paid, or should we just accept that slavery was a crime against humanity and part of the evolution of mankind, which we haven't completely evolved out of? There's slavery going on to this day. We know it exists in the Sudan, and we know of prostitution rings that force women into this line of work, as payment for bringing them to the United States, as well as other nations. Who are the slaves in the Sudan? Anyone caught believing in Jesus Christ, which makes them a Christian.

The Incompetent Politicians that are running The United States Federal Government

Chapter 6

It is amazing to me that at the height of gasoline prices, which was $4.00 per gallon, we still had politicians in Washington, D.C., arguing about the best way to solve our energy problems. Yes, gasoline is less than $4.00 per gallon, now. Should we do what the liberal Democrats want and go back to business as usual, or should we the people of the United States demand that they get out of the way and let the oil companies, drill for oil in our own country?

Yes, we do have oil companies drilling for oil in the United States, but we don't allow them to drill offshore. We do allow them to drill in federal lands, as long as they get a permit from the federal government. Usually these drilling permits, which are given to the oil companies, have little oil reserves or the oil is so hard to get to that it makes it an unprofitable situation for the oil companies. So our liberal politicians are playing politics with our security as a nation, when they give out these worthless permits. They know the oil companies won't drill for oil at a loss. We all know where the oil is in the United States. Quit with the politics; we are 70% dependent on foreign oil, start thinking about the security of our nation.

Liberal Democrats just want to ignore our energy problems. They want to put all our hopes into wind and solar power plants, which are very inefficient – just as inefficient as the federal government of the United States. How do you like that for a comparison? Liberal Democrats must think that our energy needs will go away, or that the American people will get used to high prices for fuel.

If liberal Democrats think that gasoline prices will stay below $4.00 per gallon, they're wrong. The oil-producing countries in our global markets are cutting back on their production to make fuel prices go higher. This problem won't go away, because the oil-producing nations have needs also, and want oil prices to stay at a certain level.

So who will get blamed when fuel prices go up? I believe that the Democrats should get the blame, but as usual the Democrats will blame the price increase on the Republicans. Liberal Democrats have an uncanny ability of blaming someone else for the mess, they have created. They usually get a majority of the population in the United States to believe them. This is probably why they haven't done anything about our energy crisis for 36 years.

It is unfortunate that some of the people in the United States overlook what liberal Democrats do, and let them get away with their corrupt activities. This has harmed our nation as a whole, but these same people who let the liberal Democrats have their way. Then turn around and hold the conservatives accountable for the same corrupt activities that liberal Democrats have pulled.

So when gasoline goes above $4.00 per gallon again, who are we going to hold accountable? I would think that the liberal Democrats will blame the Republicans, and the people in the United States will believe the liberal Democrats. I frankly don't understand the compassion the American people have for liberal Democrats. Liberal Democrats have knifed us in the back repeatedly, and we just stand there and take it. Some people seem to be begging for more back stabbings. I frankly don't understand it.

It is interesting to me that we have been having an argument on our energy problems for the last 36 years. Liberals have had control of Congress for a majority of these years. So what have the liberal Democrats done to solve our energy problems? As always, liberal politicians blame the people in the United States for not suffering enough, for not buying cars that couldn't hold two people comfortably. Liberals politicians say we need to conserve fuel by lowering our thermostats at home, and we should take fewer vacations to conserve our fuel. It dumbfounds me that I don't see any of these liberal Democrats doing what they are preaching.

The reason liberal Democrats aren't doing what they are preaching is because conserving fuel doesn't work. For example, we had an energy crisis back in 1973 and 1974. We only imported 24% of our oil needs. We were told to conserve fuel and we did; the thermostats in our businesses, homes and schools were lowered to 68 degrees and people cut down on the use of their cars. What happened? The energy companies complained that their profits weren't as high, therefore, they needed to raise prices, and Congress went along with the rate increases. What happened next was the oil-producing nation lifted their oil embargo and started selling oil to us again. Liberal Democrats went back to business as usual, and you are seeing the results of that today.

So why do we import 70% of our oil needs from foreign countries, instead of the 24% we imported back in the 1970s? We have roughly 100 million more people living in the United States. Let's be conservative here and say that a quarter of them own a home or rent an apartment, while the other 75 million are children to this 25 million. How many of these children go to school and how many new schools were built to educate these children? Out of these children, how many new drivers are there? Let's say that half are at driving age and half of them get a new car, paid for by their parents. So we have roughly 20 million more cars on the road. Why 20 million and not 37 million? I would think that half of these children will be driving their parents' cars. We have 25 million more homes built, new schools built, and an increase in bus usage to take the children to and from school. Does this increased use of cars, buses and home ownership have an impact on the consumption of oil? I would think so. What do you think?

I think we, the average Joe Below citizens, needs to start holding these incompetent liberal politicians accountable for their statements and actions. We need to find oil in the United States and start drilling for it, while we are developing new reusable energy sources. We need to put a timeframe to it, or the liberal Democrats will never get anything done and we will be importing 90% of our oil needs.

One of the people we need to hold accountable for his actions is Al Gore. He preaches about global warming and how we need to reduce our carbon footprint, but his carbon footprint is 20 times that of the average U.S. citizen.

The Hollywood liberals need to be held accountable. They, too, have preached about saving our environment by not allowing drilling off the shores of California, for oil, but then they turn around and drive cars that get six miles to a gallon of gasoline. Maybe we should force them to practice what they preach. Liberal Democrats have also used this line: By buying oil from the Middle East, we are sponsoring terrorists. Couldn't we say the same about them, who refuse to let us drill in the United States for our own oil, to ease the dependency on oil from the Middle East?

Liberal Democrats say that if we started drilling for oil today, we wouldn't see any benefit until 2030. I find that hard to believe, but for argument's sake, let's say that is true. So how many of us would have gone to college with that type of attitude? It takes 4 to 12 years to get out of college, depending on what degree you are going for. So you wouldn't see any benefit for your efforts until you got out of college. Do we, as a people, want these types of politicians running our country?

It doesn't matter if fuel prices go to $7.00 per gallon, for gasoline by the end of this year. What I don't like is the fact that we import 70% of our oil from nations that want to see us dead. If we do what the liberal Democrats want, by 2030 we will have done nothing and our children will be in worse shape than we are today. Do we want that?

Can't we drill and tap for our own resources in the United States and be environmentally friendly? I believe we can. I'm not a liberal Democrat who believes that we are still living in the 1950s. We as a nation have made tremendous advancements in technology. Liberal Democrats refuse to see these advancements in technology, and argue about oil spills, which will hurt our environment.

Let's drill one oil well in one of these so-called fragile environment areas, and see if we are hurting the environment. If the evidence shows that we aren't hurting the environment, then we drill more oil wells. If the evidence shows that we are, then we cap the oil well and suffer the consequences of not having enough oil to heat our homes, our businesses, fly our airplanes and drive our cars. But I believe it will show that we can do this and do it without hurting the environment.

Should we hurt our domestic automotive industries and drive cars that get 50 miles to a gallon of gasoline? The last time I looked, I didn't see any cars, our domestic automotive industries make, today, which get 50 miles to a gallon of gasoline. So that means we would have to buy foreign made cars. I don't know about other people, but I would like to support our domestic automotive industries. Not with a bailout, but by buying a fuel-efficient car. I want to be able to drive a car for more than 10 minutes before I need to get out of it because it is so uncomfortable to drive. I also don't want to live in a house without heat and air conditioning.

Other people believe that we must suffer and buy small cars, and that we should turn down our thermostats to 68 degrees. If they want to live like that, more power to them, but I don't, and I don't want to be forced to live in a society that forces people into unnecessary suffering. Do you?

I, for one, want a timeframe put on our Congress to make our country energy-independent by 2012 or 2016. If they don't, we need to vote them out of office and vote in people who understand the security of our nation is at risk, by importing 70% of our oil needs.

It Is Time to Vote for a Third Party Candidate

Chapter 7

Why is it time for moderates, independents, Reagan Democrats and conservatives to vote for third party candidates? Why do we need a viable third party in the United States? If the Republican Party can't come up with anybody better then John McCain, or the Democratic Party can't come up with anybody better then Barack Obama. Than we need to start looking for a third party candidate, who will do the will of the people of the United States.

Some people will say that both of these politicians are doing the will, of the people of the United States. I don't believe that, because both these politicians lied during their campaigns. To be elected as the next President of the United States. It doesn't surprise me to see Barack Obama do a 180 from his campaign promises.

If we can find a candidate, who will put the rights of law-abiding United States citizens above the rights of the illegal immigrants and other power corrupt people. I would vote for him/her. I for one got tired of hearing from John McCain and Barack Obama, who said we must give amnesty to illegal immigrants. These illegal immigrants have come to the United States, have stolen jobs from the citizens of this country, and have broken our laws. I'm tired of our current politicians skirting our laws and overlooking them for a political opportunity, which will increase their power and hurt the citizens of the United States in the short and long run.

I believe it's time that we send a message to Washington, which will tell our servants that we are getting tired of their corruption and their slobbering love affair with illegal immigrants. We, the law-abiding citizens of the United States, the taxpayers, are your first priority, not illegal immigrants. We need to send a message that we are getting tired of the same old disingenuous message from Democrats and Republicans, just different faces saying it. If you are tired of the same old status quo party hype, then you need to step out of the mainstream government established parties, which are the Democratic Party and the Republican Party.

So what did the candidates say? If you really listen to them, it is the same message they have been saying for the last 16 years, from Bill Clinton until George W. Bush. The message, in case you are not listening is: to grow the United States government, have the federal government intrude more into your personal lives, and have the United States government put more controls on private businesses. Socialism doesn't work. It might look good on paper, as a theory, but when it is implemented it is a dismal failure as a form of governing people.

We should allow our federal government to put some controls on our corporations, because they would run wild if we didn't. The federal government controls we have on them now, has caused a non-competitive environment. Some say unions are causing this, and that might be a factor, but since we are in a global environment, we need to give our corporations a competitive edge, not a noose around their necks with the second highest taxes in the world. If we keep going down this road we're on, more American corporations will leave our shores and go overseas to get their work done.

I wonder if the rest of the people of the United States are getting tired of the two parties we have in Washington. There pointing their fingers at each other while growing our federal government to where it takes $3.5 trillion in tax money and $1.8 trillion in deficit spending to run our federal government.

The reason I haven't asked the bleeding heart liberal Democrats to join us is because they must like high taxes. Our big, bloated, slow-moving federal government is 80% inefficient. For every dollar in taxes we pay, the federal government wastes 80 cents of it, and then 20 cents of it is put back into our economy. Now I know that there are parts of our federal government that are very efficient, such as our military, but that is one department of government that is efficient. Imagine how inefficient the other departments of the federal government of the United States have to be, to average an 80% inefficiency rating.

So that being said, I don't know about you, but I do not want the federal government of the United States getting into the health care business. If you think it is bad now, wait and see how bad it can get, when the United States government gets their hands on our health care system. How do I know this? Their track record with other government programs isn't that good. You want some examples? How about Social Security, Medicare, Medicaid and welfare.

So why didn't I vote for John McCain or Barack Obama? Well, I don't like voting for a liberal in Republican clothing or a Communist in liberal clothing. These two people have put the rights of terrorists and illegal immigrants above the rights of United States citizens. Now I know, Barack Obama is a charismatic person, but he is just too much of a Marxist for me. He wants to go overseas and talk to terrorists. He must think that he can convey an argument to them, which will make them see the light and get them to stop attacking Israel and the United States. I personally don't think it will work, but let him try and we can see if he is that naive, to believe a ruthless dictator.

I do not understand how our politicians, who are supposed to have our best interests at heart, have allowed 20 million illegal immigrants to enter the United States, and then tell the citizens of the United States that we have to give them special treatment. How many of us could steal someone's Social Security number and not get jail time for doing that? How many of us could steal someone's identity and not get jail time for that? Here's a big one: How many of us could refuse to pay taxes and not get jail time for that? Illegal immigrants have done all of this and have been offered amnesty for their law breaking because they have spent five to ten years in the United States. I find this to be amazing. Do we give bank robbers amnesty if we don't catch them in a five to ten year period? How about murderers and muggers? Do we give them amnesty if we don't catch them in a five to ten year period?

Why vote third party? Won't they become as corrupt as the politicians we have in Washington today? Yes, probably, but it will take them some time to forge alliances, to build their power base, and if they do get as corrupt as what we have in Washington today. Then we can vote them out of office too, but a three-party system may keep them honest.

A Nation Can't Survive Divided

Chapter 8

Can a nation survive divided with internal strife? The answer is no, but a nation that divides up their country, to become two or more separate nations can survive for a while before the internal strife starts up again. Many nations, which have split up their country and became separate nations, have survived for a period of time. The Western Roman Empire survived for nearly a century separated from the Eastern Roman Empire. Yes, I know that Rome had periods of reunification. Their permanent split didn't really happen until 395 A.D., which means if I go by the permanent split, they only lasted for about 80 years. The Roman Emperor Diocletian set the groundwork for the permanent split back in 285 A.D. The Western Roman Empire fell in 476 A.D., and the Eastern Roman Empire lived on, under the name of the Byzantine Empire, until the Ottoman Empire conquered them in1453 A.D.

The Greeks were split up into areas, until King Philip conquered most of Greece in 356 B.C. Most historians will tell you that the Greeks didn't agree on much of anything, Greece did come together twice and formed an alliance to keep the Persians out of their country. After the victory over the Persians, the infighting began again. The Athenian Empire was taken over by the Spartans in 404 B.C., and the Spartan Empire was defeated by the coalition of Thebes, Athens and Corinth.

The Greek Empire, after the death of Alexander the Great, was divided into four parts. You have to wonder why the Greek Empire fell apart after Alexander's death. Was Alexander the Great a tyrant, or was he well respected and with that respect, he kept his generals' loyalty? The generals of the Greek Empire split the empire into the Turkish part of Asia Minor, Egypt, Syria and Greece/Macedonia.

Israel was divided into two parts after King Solomon's death. King Solomon ruled for 40 years, and after his death "the ten northern tribes refused to submit to his son, Rehoboam and revolted."[1] So Israel and Judah were born, two separate nations ruled by two kings.

King Solomon's "downfall came in his old age," when he allowed his wives to worship false gods in Israel. [2] "He even built shrines for the sacrifices of his foreign wives."[3] In Israel under King Solomon's rule, "he placed heavy taxation on the people, who became bitter."[4] Israel became two nations. King Rehoboam ruled Judah and King Jeroboam ruled Israel. The northern kingdom (Israel) lasted for about two centuries while the southern kingdom (Judah) lasted for about three centuries.

Why write about the split-up of these three nations? They apply to our current situation. Most of the people I have talked to in the United States don't believe this will happen to us, but I wonder how many people in those countries had the same belief. So why do I think, it will happen to us? History always repeats itself. We need to understand that the United States government will have to levy heavy taxes on its population, to be able to fund all the giveaway programs the Barack Obama's administration has come up with. Will this make us bitter and angry? I think it will.

Some of the people of the United States say that the rest of the world doesn't know us and understand us. That these ancient cultures don't apply to us. I beg to differ. Human nature hasn't changed any, we have just become more knowledgeable in science and math. In a lot of cases, knowledge doesn't change behavior. Educate a barbarian and he becomes an educated barbarian. I think we need to split our nation up, mainly because of the vast differences we have in our ideals.

Why Should We Split up Our Nation?

Why should we split up the Unites States into a least four separate nations? I want to prolong our existence, even if it is by existing as separate nations. This way, at least part of the United States could survive, as the Roman Empire did. When the Western Roman Empire fell, the Eastern Roman Empire continued. I do realize that the only powerful nation, that would come out of our separation would probably be the nation run by the conservatives. All the other nations would be weak.

Why would I say such a thing? A nation that has nothing but whiners and people, who want to be taken care of, will not be strong militarily. You can see this evidence in the last days of the Western Roman Empire. A nation that puts animals and trees up to godhood will probably not be militarily strong, either. Potheads will be too busy smoking pot or taking other drugs to care about anything else.

Our infighting and internal strife will lead to our eventual destruction as a nation. Jesus said a kingdom cannot stand divided. Historians have said the same thing: a nation cannot stand divided. When a nation is split up into the factions that cause internal strife, the nation will become many separate nations and survive until the internal strife starts again. This infighting might be stopped if we allow open borders for the people to cross if their political philosophy would deem it so. This might stop the internal strife, or at least slow it down.

What Nation Would Survive

What nation would survive if we allowed this to happen? I think the conservative nation would be one. They probably would prosper and be strong militarily. I believe that hard work would make the difference between the nations. I feel that the conservative nation would reward the people who had such a work ethic. The people who overcome the bigotry of another through hard work, instead of bellyaching about being discriminated against are the backbone of a nation. It is unfortunate that people hold such hatreds for another human being, but it goes on. I'm discriminated against every day, either through jealousy or because of my ideals. You see, I'm not a liberal, so I can see the hatred from some of them, and especially when they learn that I'm a Christian.

I have noticed several things about liberal Democrats. They believe that only they have the right to speak and only they have the answers to our problems. They also believe that the people of the United States are too stupid to know what's good for them. So in their arrogance, liberal Democrats feel that they should decide what's best for us.

I became an adult when I reached the age of 18, and I don't need the liberal Democratic Party to make my decisions for me. I don't want to be their tax base for their social programs. I don't want laws passed because they feel that I'm going to hurt myself. This is why I have become an Independent.

People, who are Independents, would have to decide which nation to live in. I would choose the conservative nation. The reasoning behind my decision is I don't think the government can solve all our problems. I think given the chance, people can do a better job. I feel that in some cases, the federal government with its meddling has actually intensified the problems. I believe the conservatives when they say that our taxes are too high, and that we don't have an income problem but a liberal Democrat base spending problem. Unlike Tom Daschle, I don't think that raising taxes is the answer to every problem we have as a nation. I don't believe that throwing money at a problem will always be the solution to our problems. Unlike liberal Democrats, I don't feel that I should be held accountable for what my father, grandfather or great-grandfather has done.

Another reason the United States should split up into many nations is because of the ideals of the people of this country. The ideals of liberal and conservative people are so different that you are seeing the destruction of our nation being played out. You're seeing partisanship brought to a new level by Barack Obama. When a nation has such strife between its people, it doesn't have long to exist. A similar nation that had this kind of strife was the Ming Dynasty. Their nation fell to the Manchurians.

Does it Matter How We Split up the Country

Does it matter how we split our nation up? It could, if you would want to have borders. Then we would need to split the country up, by north, south, east and west. The way I would do it is without borders between the nations, as far as the people go. They should have the right to go back and forth between the nations, as they please. The people who think they are entitled to something could form the liberal nation alliance. The people who feel an animal is their god can form the nation of animal rights, while environmentalists who believe that a tree is their god can form the environmentalist nation. Drug users can form the pothead nation, where all the druggies can go.

Who should move to the liberal nation? The ones who want to live off the hard work of another. The people who feel that a segment of our society should be taken care of, or be given slave reparations because they feel guilty for what their ancestors did, over 140 years ago. The people who think, the federal government can solve all our problems and who want the working people to be the tax base.

The people who want to stand on their own two feet can form the conservative nation. Who should move to the conservative nation? The people who want to have less government in their lives. The people who want to have competition put back into our schools. The people who want to pay fewer taxes and have their freedoms restored. The people who feel they have the right to correct their children without government intervention. This should be allowed, providing that they use a certain amount of restraint in the disciplining of their children. The people who want to make their own decisions, when it comes to their lives and their families.

Who should move to the animal rights nation? People who believe that an animal is their god or have the belief that animals have the same rights as human beings do. Who should move to the environmentalist nation? Anyone who feels we should live in harmony with nature and wants to live in caves underground or feels you should run around naked. Anyone who worships a tree as their god should go there.

British India split up into many nations because of the internal strife between the Muslims and the Hindus. The split-up of British

India started when India was given independence from Britain. The internal strife in British India was there when Britain had them as a colony. The British had managed to keep everything under control, but once India was given independence, the internal strife could not be contained. We know the result of their internal strife. Their split-up was caused by a difference in religions, while ours would be caused by a difference in ideologies.

Inconsistencies and Double Standards within Our Laws and Our Society

Chapter 9

Will inconsistencies in our laws bring internal strife? Will inconsistencies intensify our internal strife? The answer to both of these questions is yes. Why yes? It is due to our human nature. There are people who get highly offended when they see an unfairness done to someone. These people don't realize that the world is unfair.

The Civil Rights laws that were passed in the 1960s didn't get rid of the "good old boy" system. It's still alive and doing quite well. We see this part of our human nature in our children. How many parents can say that they saw their children fighting over an unfairness done to them, because one child supposedly got a better Christmas present? How many of us have seen this? A person getting upset when they feel that they should have gotten the promotion that someone else did. She/he, then sets out on a seek-and-destroy mission, and will do almost anything to make sure this person fails in his attempt to succeed.

Inconsistency in our laws will happen when a law is passed by an emotional outburst by liberal Democrats. We have just recently seen one of these outbursts by the liberal Democratic Party in Washington. They started their spiels about a 90% tax levied on the banking executives who received any bonuses of $1 million or more. Of course, this only applied to the banks that took bailout money.

The banks that were forced to take this bailout money wanted to pay it back, due to the emotional outburst of these liberal Democrats, and also because they didn't want the federal government dictating to them, how they should run their businesses. The federal government, at first refused to accept the money, because it seems that our federal government wants to nationalize our banking industry.

Even more inconsistencies occur when we pass laws for political reasons or because it feels right. Our laws should be based on the need to stop injustices. These laws need to be well thought out and passed because it is the right thing to do, not because it will bring a politician political power. Inconsistencies also happen when judges feel that they can legislate from the bench. Laws should be passed by our legislative branch, the branch that represents the people, not the judicial branch that cannot be held accountable by the people.

There are some laws that are passed, which make certain behavior illegal because the federal government can't or won't take tax revenue from these activities. If the federal government is acting on a moral basis, then I agree with their decision, but in most cases the decision-making is based on political advancement. They will come up with something to make it illegal if it doesn't give them some kind of political advantage.

Where has there been some inconsistency in our laws? How about Timothy Geithner, a tax cheat who should have gotten jail time but got a job as the Secretary of the Treasury in the United States federal government? Pete Rose was said to be a tax cheat; he got 18 months in jail. How about Wesley Snipes? As far as I know, he was sentenced to three years in jail. This is kind of interesting to me. If you are a liberal Democrat and your buddy is Barack Obama, you can be a tax cheat and be rewarded by the President of the United States, with one of the top-level position in the federal government. They said they were going to get rid of the "good old boy" system? That will be the day.

Here's another one: if a man kills a woman who is pregnant, he is charged with two murders; one for the woman and another one for the unborn child. But a woman can have an abortion and it is not considered murder. I believe the man should be charged with two homicides because I believe that the unborn child is a living being. So why isn't the woman, who had an abortion charged with murder? Didn't she take the life of her unborn child, just as the man did when he killed the pregnant woman? Do we charge the man with two murders because we want to assume that the woman wanted to keep the baby?

I hope that someone is not trying to argue that the woman has a right to decide, to have an abortion, based on it being her body and she can do what she wants with it. If that were so, that you can do anything you want with your body, then why don't we allow people to sell their body parts, to the highest bidder? We have passed laws contrary to the belief that you can do anything you want with your body, as long as it doesn't affect someone else's body. The law that forbids people to sell their body parts was passed, not on the basis of morals, but based on insurance issues.

Lawmakers felt that insurance costs would skyrocket if this was allowed. This might be true, considering that a man went on eBay during the Clinton's presidency to sell his kidney and was offered $5 million for it.

One interesting inconsistency in our society is how we, within a 20-year period, went from outrage to "its okay, it's only about sex." Bill Clinton wasn't impeached for being a sex deviant or an adulterer. What he was impeached for was obstruction of justice. We were outraged in the 1970s with what Richard Nixon did. What Richard Nixon did was basically the same as what Bill Clinton did. Richard Nixon covered up the Watergate break-in. This was obstruction of justice. So why bring this up? Just to show you how far, liberal Democrats have managed to destroy our moral values.

China had Double Standards like we have Today in the United States

Our nation is not the first nation to have double standards. Every nation on the face of the Earth has had one form or another of double standards. Is having double standards a natural part of the human character? I believe that it is. Double standards have caused nations to fall, have caused internal strife in nations, and have caused countries to become corrupt through their leaders' double standards. It has caused slavery and the holocaust of countless people. Bigotry is a form of a double standard.

Why would anyone think we would be different? The answer I come up with is: the hope that we would be different because of our heritage. This answer I came up with is, because the people of the United States came from all the countries in the world that practiced slavery, bigotry, and cruelty. I was hoping that we the people of the United States would have learned from our ancestors, who came from these nations, but some people who fought their way to the top only invoke their own double standards. Slavery, bigotry, and cruelty were and still are a way of life to some people in the United States. Not all the people of our country practice these double standards, but double standards do exist, and it seems that the liberal Democrats of the United States are the worst of the worst, when it comes to having an agenda on double standards.

They have implemented a system loaded with double standards, which they say is good legislation for the people of the United States. If you disagree, you suddenly have your character destroyed and have all kinds of politically incorrect allegations thrown at you. So you mustn't question their system of double standards. This system of double standards liberal Democrats have created falls under the protection of the political correctness doctrine.

The liberal Democrats' system of double standards says, "We can do it, but you can't. We can lie, cheat, deceive, mislead, scheme, plot, connive and break the law, but you can't." The embodiment of this is Bill Clinton, and now it seems to be Barack Obama, but I think Barack Obama will be worse because he has a messiah complex and some people seem to worship him.

So how did we get to this point, to where we have allowed someone to implement these types of double standards? Why have we closed our eyes to it? We closed our eyes to it because the politicians, who implemented this, gave us, what we wanted and as long as we get what we want, we forget about everybody else. The double standards system is also called politics. Its politics to let someone live off the hard work of another, and its politics to give someone a free education who hasn't earned it, but everybody else has to pay for it.

I can go on forever about the political double standards, but I want to give you an example of the political correctness double standards. Although some people have said that political correctness is really justification for lying, I'm not sure that political correctness is that. What we have done, is we have allowed the political correctness nerds to put labels on us, and if we object to these labels, we are viewed as intolerant. You will also receive condemnation from them, because you didn't like their label. They will say something like this: Do you know how long it took me to come up with that label? No, I don't know, and I don't care, either.

When someone else puts a label on someone that doesn't fall under the political correctness doctrine, you are a bigot, a racist, a homophobe, or sexist. You see, political correctness is a system that forces you to think a certain way. So when you question the actions of these thought police, they get upset.

If you and your buddy come up with a nickname for each other and it falls outside the political correctness doctrine, you can be expelled from college or lose your job. How is this? Well, the thought police go and complain about your use of this nickname, which you gave your buddy, and how they were deeply offended by your actions. Instead of the school principal or the human resources manager telling them to get out of their office, they call you and your buddy in for disciplinary action.

When did our double standards start? I believe they started back at the beginning of Adam's and Eve's fall from God's grace, when they were told to leave the Garden of Eden. Double standards have been alive and doing quite well ever since.

Now when did double standards get started in our country? I believe it started back when people left Great Britain. These people were forced by the King, to worship in a religion that was contrary to their beliefs. They wanted to worship freely the God of their choice. You see in England, you had to belong to the Church of England or face persecution, even execution. So the persecuted left and finally came here to start over and worship as they pleased.

Double standards slowly crept into our society until liberal politicians got control and then the floodgates were opened. I wonder if our forefathers are turning over in their graves now, seeing the same double standard implemented by the liberal Democrats in the United States. Liberal Democrats are now indoctrinating our children into the religions of Atheism, Darwinism and any religion that is anti-Christian. The children are learning this in our government-run school system.

So why am I talking about liberal Democrats who have implemented these double standards, if every nation on the face of the earth has had them? Why am I talking about the anti-Christian liberal organizations that are fighting a war against Christianity? In case you haven't noticed, they're winning this war. Have the liberal politicians joined force with Al Qaeda? I don't believe they have, but it makes you wonder, especially when they consistently badmouth our military personnel by calling them murderers and Nazis.

I think liberal Democrats want us to be like China. It's not against the law to be Christian in China, as long as you don't tell anyone. As soon as a Chinese Christian tells someone that he is a Christian, he is persecuted for his beliefs by the Chinese government. Liberal Democrats have organizations that are waging a war against Christian values, which are moral philosophies set down by Jesus Christ. This war is basically against any of the philosophies that will make you a responsible person with discipline, which will make you a decent, productive member of our society. They want a deviant society, where they call all the shots. Sodom and Gomorrah would be tame in comparison, or would be the moral capital of the world if liberal Democrats get their way. In other words, they want a world that the anti-Christ would be proud of.

China's dynasties had double standards like ours; they had slavery, discrimination and laws that only applied to the peasantry. Laws didn't apply to the emperors of China. The emperors could do whatever they wanted to and weren't punished for breaking the laws of China. The rich that had the political favor of the emperor, or were the authority of a town or a city could basically do whatever they wanted, without any worries from the magistrates. If any sentencing was carried out, the penalty was insignificant to the people of privilege.

This sounds a lot like Bill Clinton. He got an insignificant sentence by the liberal judges he appointed. If liberal Democrats receive punishment for their law breaking, it is usually a light sentence. As long as you are a liberal Democrat elitist, laws do not apply to you. Timothy Geithner is another example.

How did we as a nation get to the point where we let people off, when we know and have proof they have broken the law? Why do we allow liberal Democrats to break the law, at will, and think its okay, but hold everyone else who aren't liberal Democrat elitists to the letter of the law? Why have we allowed liberal judges to circumvent the law? When liberal judges don't uphold the law of the land, they dodge the law by calling it unconstitutional but totally ignore the Constitution when it suits them.

The judges I'm talking about are the judges that legislate from the bench and totally ignore the law. Two examples have been reported on the Bill O'Reilly TV news hour. One of these judges is in Chicago. She aided a felon by having him escorted out of her courtroom by her guards, then taken through her judge chambers and put on the judges' elevator and let go. The police had an arrest warrant, which she knew about. In legal terms, isn't this referred to as aiding and abetting a felon, which is jail time for us commoners? Why wasn't she arrested? Why isn't she on trial for aiding and abetting a felon? Is it because she is part of the elite liberal judge system?

The other example is a judge in New York. He refused to have a mayor arrested for breaking the state law of New York by performing same sex marriages. This judge instead said the law was unconstitutional. This law might very well be, but he didn't have the authority to make that call. Once a law has been voted in by the people of that state, it takes the Supreme Court of that state to determine if that law is unconstitutional. If the law is unconstitutional, then the courts have to put a stay on that law.

China's Neolithic to the Xia Dynasty

Chapter 10

The history of the Chinese people started back about 14,000 years ago, although the nation of China wasn't formed until the Xia Dynasty came into existence in 2100B.C. But there were nomadic tribes in the area. "The Neolithic period began in China about 12,000 B.C."[1] Some historians say that China has about 4,000 years of history, the second oldest culture in the world. However, the Chinese people say they have 5,000 years of history, still the second oldest culture in the world. The Middle East is considered to have the oldest culture on the face of the Earth.

In China's rich history of 5,000 years, China has had numerous wars, rebellions, culture achievements, has split up into different kingdoms, and has had at least four forms of government. The Dynasty form of government was the longest-lasting type of government China has had.

The United States is a baby in comparison to China. We have 228 to 400 years of history, depending on where you want to start our existence. I usually start ours at the end of the Revolutionary War. Some will argue that I should start at the time the pilgrims landed at Plymouth Rock. The reason I don't believe we should start our history, as a nation, and then is because we weren't a nation. We were a group of colonies and eventually became a colony to the British Empire (England).

The Dynasty style of government was started in the Xia Dynasty, but this wasn't their first type of government. The abdication style of government was used until Xia Yu Di's son broke up that system. Bo Yi was supposed to be the successor to Xia Yu Di by Xia Yu Di's abdication. As usual in this type of government, what one king or emperor wants doesn't always happen. Usually the one with the most power won the throne.

There's some discrepancy here. Some historians say that the dukes voted Xia Qi in as king and then had Bo Yi killed. "According to the 'Bamboo Annals,' however, Bo Yi took the throne and became King of China, but later Qi assassinated him and abducted the throne."[2] However it came about, Xia Qi got to the throne and became king. Due to this, China's dynasty era got started. The dynasty form of government is the longest-lasting type of government, known to mankind. It still exists in some parts of the world today.

There are historians who say that the Xia Dynasty was the first dynasty to start slavery. When Xia Qi became king; "Qi used his position of power to" implement a policy of forced labor, thus establishing slavery in China. [3]

I understand that China became a slave-based nation from that point in time, but you can still have a society based on slavery with many different types of governments. The United States had slavery and still does to this day. We are supposed to be a Republic, and in our Declaration of Independence we say that all men are created equal, but we still put other men/women into bondage. In our Constitution, we say that a Black man is only three-fifths of a man. This was done to stop the rich Southern people, who owned slaves from stuffing the ballet box, during elections years, which would affect the outcome at state and local levels.

The slavery we have today is just a different form than what some people think, when they hear the word slavery. We have sex slavery, slave labor, and people who were put into slavery by the politicians in our country. The politicians created a form of slavery called welfare, which put the people who receive this aid under the control of the federal government. Refer to chapter 4. People who pay taxes are slaves to the United States government as a tax base, and find that they have to work for half of a year, to pay their tax burden.

If historians are trying to say that people were slaves to the ruling family, that is true, but China still could have had slavery under the abdication form of government. It just would have been under many different kings and emperors, rather than just under a ruling family style of government. China today has slavery; we call this form slave labor. It's interesting that China started their slavery policies 4,000 years ago. Slave labor is still practiced in the United States. It is illegal, but you have to catch them. Sweat shops throughout our country have been reported to exist. Do we try to stop it? Yes, but it still goes on.

The Xia Dynasty, to some historians, is not "accepted as a true dynasty," but for lack of a better term, let's call it that for the time being. [4] "The people of the Xia Dynasty were agrarian type people."[5] They believed in socialism (liberalism), which to them meant the equal distribution of land in the interest of promoting agricultural. Is promoting a nice way of saying forced? If they were true liberal Democrats, it would be forced. Liberal Democrats are highly intolerant when it comes to someone having a different opinion, ideals or wanting to do something different than what they want.

I'm sure that China's form of socialism (liberalism) was corrupted, to the same extent as ours is today. In our case, the corruption is caused by the liberal Democrats we have in the United States government. In the Xia Dynasty's case, the king or chieftain caused most of the corruption by getting most, if not all, of the crops through taxation.

We have the same situation in our country too. The liberal Democrats drive around in limos and many other types of vehicles that are considered gas guzzlers, but then turn around and tell us that you can't drive these types of vehicles. Liberal Democrats such as Barack Obama, after earning millions of dollars, then turn around and tell us to work for a nonprofit organization. This liberal elitism is nauseating to me, but what do you expect from the party of double standards?

It is interesting to know that liberalism was utilized 4,000 years ago in the Xia Dynasty. I wonder if people will ever evolve from elitism, mooching and non-caring instincts. Not all people have these characteristics, but a lot of us do, and it seems the liberal Democrats in power definitely have utilized this flaw in our character.

It seems there are some people who feel they are better than others; usually these types of people turn to the liberal viewpoint and tell everyone else, "do what I say, not as I do." They go around telling everybody what they should do, but they don't practice what they preach. A few examples of elitists would be Hilary Clinton, Barbara Streisand, Bill Clinton and Barack Obama. Barack Obama is an elitist, but he seems to have a messianic complex, too, which in his thinking would make him an elitist to the elites.

Barbara Streisand drives an RV around Hollywood that gets six miles to a gallon of gasoline, but then turns around and tells us we can't drive SUVs because of the poor gasoline miles. If you asked her about her hypocritical viewpoint, I believe she would say something like this: I should be allowed to drive this vehicle because I'm somebody and you're not.

Bill Clinton broke the laws of our country, and felt that his actions should be ignored, that he did nothing wrong, while the rest of us would have been put in jail for 7 to 10 years for the same crime. Hilary Clinton feels that only she has the right to freedom of speech. This became obvious during her 2000 campaign run for the Senate seat in New York. "A former advance man for New York Sen. Hilary Clinton has confessed that her campaign used 'etiquette squads' to drive hecklers away at rallies."[6]

This doesn't surprise me, considering that Hilary Clinton is a liberal elitist. I would expect her to have etiquette squads (goon squads) that would be sent out to shut up hecklers and have a few reporters roughed up. After all, only liberals are allowed to have the First Amendment rights of freedom of speech. It is also apparent that when she fought to become an elitist in the United States, she wasn't going to bring anyone up with her.

In my opinion, she wanted peasants to worship her as the empress of New York, and now wants us to give her that same status as Secretary of State. I wonder what kind of deal was made behind the scenes between Hilary Clinton and Barack Obama, for Hilary to get the job of Secretary of State.

It's interesting about elitism. There have been elitists in the past that have pulled their country up with them during their climb to the elite status. There have been some elitists that only care about themselves, such as Hilary Clinton, and have only pull themselves up. There have been some cases where people who have reached the elite status have actually destroyed their country or dynasty, such as King Jie.

We the people of the United States, at the beginning of our nation, enjoyed the elitists who brought our country up with them. However now, we have elitists like Hilary Clinton who feel that only she should be an elitist. What happened to the elitists that brought their country up with them? Well, that's easy, a certain type of liberal started to fight to get to the elite status in the 1960s, and in spite of what everyone thinks, these types of liberals only care about themselves.

It seems that these elitists have their hearts set on destroying the United States, or at least bring the United States down to a semi-colonial power controlled by the United Nations. I believe that the liberal elitists that started their climb to power had a total hatred for the United States in the 1960s, and they still seem to have it today. Instead of changing our country for the better under their elitism, it seems that they have destroyed our culture, our morals and our honesty.

Mooching and freeloading seems to fall under the protection of the liberal agenda. These types of people that suck blood, feel that the world owes them, and they find ways to be supported by the hard work of others. Our federal government aids these free-spirited people by plundering the working class through taxation. Usually, people who try to get someone else to support them do not advance in our society. These types of people usually stay down at the bottom of the economic ladder and whine, moan, grumble and complain about how they weren't given a fair chance.

Some of these people have made bad decisions in their lives and don't want to correct that decision. Others were just too lazy to try. This type of person feels that others should take care of him/her. If you want to be a bum and live off the charity of others, then that is up to you and that person who wants to take care of you. The federal government of the United States, on the other hand, does not have the right to force charitable contributions. The federal government of the United States doesn't have the right to plunder the producers and give it to the non-producers, as Barack Obama wants to do.

The freeloaders and people who support them want to empower our federal government, to plunder the producers in the United States. Usually people who want to be taken care of have this type of mentality: If I can't make it, then no one else should either.

I hope that we don't develop the attitude of the citizenry of the USSR. A peasant in Russia had a question put to him. The question was this: I will give you whatever you ask for, but I will give your neighbor double. The peasant's reply was: Take out one of my eyes and half my teeth. Liberals love these types of people with this type of character flaw. They know that they can get them to become part of the Democratic Party and vote for their agenda. All they have to do is just pass more laws, which are designed to plunder the producers, and then take their ill-gotten gains (spoils) and give it to the non-producers in the United States. This is liberalism at its worst.

Liberal Democrats in their attempt to redistribute wealth, which was also done in the Xia Dynasty, usually use a variety of ploys and deception to maintain the support of these freeloaders. This is usually done for political expediency. The politician's sell the producers down the river, to give to the non-producers. This creates class warfare because the producers want to know, why they have to work hard to support their families and why do the non-producers get a free ride, at their expense? Liberals love class warfare, because it puts people at odds with each other, which keeps, the attention off of them.

It's kind of interesting how liberal Democrats have created the illusion that they are the party that cares for others, while in reality they only care about power, which is done by subjugating a certain type of people.

The Xia Dynasty Conquered

The Xia dynasty lasted for 439 years, if you go by the year it supposedly started in 2205 B.C. and the supposed year it ended, in 1766 B.C. But some say that they lasted either 431 years or 471years. This is interesting. I've seen this with the Zhou and the Qin Dynasties, different accounts as to how long they actually existed.

I wonder if the leaders Of the Xia Dynasty knew they were going to fall, or did they put a blind eye to the inevitable as we are doing today? So why did the Xia Dynasty fall? "The fall of the Xia Dynasty is blamed on its last king, Jie, who is said to have fallen in love with an evil, beautiful woman and become a tyrant."[7] Xia Jie also lived for enjoyment. It seemed that he didn't care about the people or the state of affairs, which ended in his eventual exile and the defeat of the dynasty. He paid no heed to the unrest and the outside aggressors threatening his kingdom.

As the internal strife was mounting along with the outside aggressors, it seems that it was only a matter of time. So did he know and didn't care, or was he like the liberal Democrats of the United States? The liberal Democrats in the United States look at every event as a political benefit or as a political disadvantage. I believe that liberal Democrats are exactly like this king; they live for power and will do whatever it takes to get it.

The last king of the Xia Dynasty didn't know that his kingdom didn't have long to exist. When one of his ministers warned him that his extravagance would doom the dynasty, and that he needed to pay more attention to the state of affairs. He just laughed and said: I am like the sun; "will the sun be extinguished."[8] So he went on with his enjoyments with the time he had left. I wonder if he was like the liberal Democrats in our country, thinking that he could appease the aggressors and they would leave him and his kingdom alone. Did he think as liberal Democrats do today that the peril wasn't real? I think for sure that his lifestyle took precedence over his kingdom's security. In our country, liberal Democrats' social programs take precedence over everything, especially our nation's security and military.

It's not clear why Xia Jie was a tyrant, but it is believed it was because of Mei Xi, his royal concubine. "Mei Xi was beautiful but wicked."[9] "It is commonly believed that she was largely responsible for the downfall of the Xia Dynasty."[10] I wonder if this was her plan from the beginning. After all, she was given to Jie as a peace settlement.

King Jie the tyrant "amused himself and his wife by ordering 3000 people to kill themselves by jumping into a lake of wine."[11] Extra taxes were levied onto the population to meet Jie and Mei Xi's needs for pleasure. Naturally this brought bitterness and hatred to the population. As the hatred grew among the population, so did the strength of the vassal state of Shang.

Jie ordered the execution of Guan Longfeng, a minister who was sickened by his behavior. Guan went to the king with a scroll and read from it. Guan's argument with the king was based on his behavior. The scroll that Guan read from, described how the first king cared about his subjects, and that King Jie should change his ways and be more attentive to his subjects. This naturally threw Jie into a rage. "Guan continued to argue with Jie until he was taken out and beheaded."[12]

Historians say that King Jie became a tyrant because of his wife. Men do a lot of strange things to please their women. However, he must have had that personality trait, for him to become a tyrant. His wife just brought it out of him. What I believe is he became a tyrant due to the power that he accumulated and due to his royal concubine. No one will know for sure, but it led to his fall and the destruction of his family's dynasty.

If Mei Xi was a tyrant in her own right, she was still a concubine. The decision-making was done by the king. The king could have said no to her desires. He could have put a stop to all the outrageous events, to bring pleasure to him and his concubine. It's not like she could have left him for someone else.

Shang Tang, who was supposed to be a man of virtue and wisdom, overthrew the Xia Dynasty. Shang Tang's forces surrounded Xia Jie and efficiently defeated him. "Shang Tang exiled Xia Jie to Nanchao."[12] When Shang Tang was offered the imperial seal, he turned down the offer three times, but finally accepted. So did Mei Xi go with Xia Jie into exile?

We do have it a little bit different here in the United States, but our destruction will occur from our pleasure seeking. Our pleasure-seeking opportunities have made us complacent. We have developed apathy, to the events around us, and care more about who's going to win American Idol. Than what is happening in Washington with our elected servants. Now the question is: Were we maneuvered into our apathy, or did we develop it?

The Xia Dynasty to the Shang and Zhou Dynasties

Chapter 11

The Shang Dynasty overthrew the Xia Dynasty and became the second dynasty of China. Some historians still hold the Shang Dynasty as the "first true dynasty of China."[1] The history of China points out that the last emperor of the Xia Dynasty of China was a tyrant and that the Xia Dynasty became weak, due to his appetite for pleasure. In studying history, one must remember that the victors write the history. Historians will always tell you that sometimes, history is written to justify the actions of one group over another. In some cases that of an individual. Written history has to be taken with caution, because people who write the history of their country have emotions and agendas. We are seeing that today with Bill Clinton.

Xia Jie the last king of the Xia Dynasty reminds me of Bill Clinton. Although I do not know if Bill Clinton is a tyrant, I do know that Bill Clinton is a pleasure-seeking animal that allowed our country to become weak, under his watch. His lack of concern for our security and his soft approach on terrorism caused our current situation and the attack on September 11, 2001. Now we have Barack Obama, a man who probably will be worse than Bill Clinton. I do think that both of these men need to be given the Neville Chamberlain award for being so naive. Maybe we should just say that Bill Clinton makes Jimmy Carter and Richard Nixon look good and leave it at that, or should we rate Jimmy Carter's and Richard Nixon's presidencies to see where Bill Clinton would fall. We will have to wait before we can determine where Barack Obama will fall, but if he doesn't change his perspectives, he will replace Bill Clinton as the worst president this country has ever had.

Now back to Jimmy Carter and Richard Nixon. If there was a poll taken and one of the questions would ask you, to rank Jimmy Carter against the other men who were presidents of the United States in the 20th century, how would he be ranked? Well, until Bill Clinton came along, he would have been ranked last.

Now Jimmy Carter would be ranked second to last, while Richard Nixon would be ranked third to last, bringing Bill Clinton in last. Now if another question was asked to rate Jimmy Carter's presidency, how would his be rated? Well, if the questionnaire was ranked as excellent, good, fair or poor, I believe most people in my age group would cross out poor and write in rotten. The one thing that makes Jimmy Carter a better President than Bill Clinton is that Jimmy Carter is considered to be an honorable man. I don't know if that is true. I never met the man.

One mannerism of liberal Democrats that I have noticed is this: The more of a failure you are, the more prestige you have among their ranks. Jimmy Carter was a big failure as a president, but is rated highly among liberal Democrats. Bill Clinton had a mediocre to rotten presidency, but is also rated highly among them. Al Gore is another example of a failure, and he is rated highly. Al Gore was the court jester of the Clinton's administration and continues to be an imbecile. He now takes his act of global warming around the world.

The rewriting of our history has happened quite often, but I don't think the past rewrites have been anything like what we're seeing today with Bill Clinton's presidency. They're doing everything they can to try to make Bill Clinton's presidency look good, but it is hard for them to rewrite history when so many of us are still alive, to set the record straight. What they should do is to try to rewrite the history on Bill Clinton when this generation passes away. Bill Clinton was a mediocre to rotten president, and if history is written accurately, it will point this out in time.

Liberal Democrats hope that the people of the United States have short memories. I say that Bill Clinton was a mediocre to rotten president. To back up my claim, all you have to do is walk up to any sane individual and ask this question: Can you name me anything good that Bill Clinton did for our country or for the people, in his eight years as president? I usually get an answer like this: "He did a lot of things." Really, can you be more specific, like naming me any programs that benefited the people or the country? I usually get the same answer: "He did a lot of things." Well, I can't name anything good that Bill Clinton did for our country, but I can name many things he did to our country and to us.

The things Bill Clinton did to our country and to the people will take a generation to correct. So what did he do? He raised taxes on the working people of this country; Barack Obama wants to do the same. This will intensify the vicious cycle that was put into place by Lyndon Baines Johnson. When liberal Democrats raise our taxes, it means that we the taxpayers have to work more hours to replace the disposable income that has been taken away from us, by the federal government. This in turn affects the family, which means that the mothers and fathers have less time to spend with their children, thus causing the breakdown of the family structure even more. With this happening in our society; this leaves the children to grow up without a father and mother. This causes the children to need more federal government social programs, now and down the road, which means taxes will have to be increased to fund these new federal government social programs, which will again intensify this vicious cycle.

Was this a liberal Democrat's ploy to cause our children to need federal government programs? Was it a liberal Democrat's strategy, so that these children will not have a mother and father in their lives? So they wouldn't get the nurturing from the mother and the discipline from the father, which will make them a responsible adult? Were these tax increases used by the liberal Democrats to make sure that parents who have children, who go to school wouldn't have the time to check up on them, to make sure they're getting a decent education?

No matter what Bill Clinton and the Democrats say, Clinton's tax increase on only the top one percent of wage earners was really a tax across the board, and now Barack Obama wants to increase the tax rate on the top five percent of wage earners. We'll just have to wait and see if it will be the same, which will hurt all the working people in the United States. Liberal Democrats must believe that a big, bloated, slow-moving federal government made our country great. What made our country great was the American family, which has been under attack by the liberal Democrats for a long time, and we are starting to see the results of their efforts.

What Bill Clinton did to our country was to weaken our military to the point that we had to wait twenty some odd months before we could attack Iraq, and even then we didn't have enough military supplies and manpower in the country to restore order. Bill Clinton reduced the budget for the CIA, and we wonder why we got such poor intelligence from this agency. Liberal Democrats have justified these reductions in the CIA's budget by saying our spy satellite system will take care of it.

Bill Clinton had his administration build a wall between the federal intelligent agencies and law enforcement, and we wonder why there wasn't any communication between these organizations. Liberal Democrats just don't understand, or they don't want to understand, that our spy satellite system is good for checking out facilities. It can't help you find spies or terrorists. Only men and women on the ground in enemy countries can do that.

One must ask why Bill Clinton reduced the CIA budget. The first priority of a government official is to keep our country safe. So why did Bill Clinton do this? The money that was saved from the CIA and military budgets was diverted to his social programs. One should remember that social programs are good to a point, but should never be budgeted to the point that a nation's security is threatened, and that is exactly what Bill Clinton and his administration did.

So why did Bill Clinton do it? I think it was done to shore up his voting base and to get the people who were pulling themselves out of poverty back into poverty. You see, once someone doesn't need your help, and finds out that he/she can make it on their own, you then know that you will lose his/her support, especially when they make it to the taxpaying rolls of our society. This is way we have spent $9 trillion on failed federal government programs. They were never designed to fix the problem.

There's one thing Bill Clinton can boast about: he didn't go along with John Kerry's plan to reduce the CIA's budget even further by an additional $6 billion, right after the first Twin Towers attack. I will give Bill Clinton credit for that.

Internal Strife of a Country

If King Jie of the Xia Dynasty was a tyrant, he paid the price for ignoring the internal strife of his country. King Jie, did he ignore the internal affairs of the state because he had a lack of understanding for politics? Have our government officials paid the price for their arrogance and lack of insight on terrorism?

I don't believe they have paid a price, but I know we the people have paid and will pay again, do to their ineptness. So who would I get rid of? I would get rid of anyone in our Congress who voted to reduce the budget of the military and of the CIA. How should we get rid of them? It's very easy, vote them out of office. Anyone like Ted Kennedy should be voted out of public office.

Did the last king of the Xia Dynasty put people that he trusted in charge of his dynasty? It appears that he didn't, but if he did, then he should have taken sometime out of his pleasure-seeking schedule to see if the people, he trusted, were worthy of his trust.

In the Clinton administration, did Bill Clinton put people in charge he trusted while he was seeking pleasure for himself? Maybe he should have taken some time out of his pleasure-seeking schedule and seen how his people were doing.

One must ask, is this part of human nature? Do people become corrupt, lazy, and complacent while their nation is the superpower of the world? When a country rises to power, the people in charge usually start out with benevolent behavior to the peasants. As time passes, and generation after generation of the same family stays in power, they slowly become corrupt or inept. I believe the Kennedy clan would be a good example of this.

I believe that some people put into a position of authority over people and country eventually become corrupt, lazy, complacent and inept. This is why I'm for putting term limits on our politicians who want to run for public office in our country. The United States doesn't have one family running the federal government affairs, but it seems that we constantly elect the same type of people, to public office, which gives them power and wealth, which in turn leads them down the path to corruption.

The Beginning of the Shang Dynasty

As Chinese history states, a man named Shang Tang was "a man of great virtue and wisdom," he believed in treating people benevolently. [2] Shang Tang took advantage of the situation the Xia Dynasty was in and launched his attack. In his victory over the Xia Dynasty, he became the first emperor of the Shang Dynasty, which lasted for 649 years. History points out that the last Emperor of the Shang Dynasty was a tyrant.

It seems that King Di Xin (Zhou) and Da Ji history is almost identical to the history of King Jie and Mei Xi. King Zhou went out to conquer "the state of You Su and took Da Ji as his trophy."[3] King Zhou would do anything to please Da Ji. They also had a pond of wine and meat hanging from trees around the pond.

"Da Ji was best known for her invention of a device of torture called Paolao" also known as the cannon burning punishment.[4] As King Zhou became obsessed with Da Ji, he ignored the affairs of the state and of the people. He also had to levy heavy taxes on the people to pay for Da Ji's amusement.

Historians of today don't believe that King Zhou and Da Ji did all the atrocities history claims. They feel that it could have been "a propaganda ploy on the part of the Zhou tribe."[5] Why would the tribe of the Zhou come up with such a ploy? This could have been done for justification to overthrow the Shang Dynasty. If Da Ji was not the evil wicked woman of the Shang Dynasty, then she was demonized by the Zhou tribe to rally support around them. If this was the case "then Da Ji would have been the victim of the first psychological warfare that history has ever seen."[6] It seemed to have worked, because the army of the Shang Dynasty joined forces with the tribes of Zhou to overthrow King Di Xin (Zhou).

Who uses psychological warfare today? I would have to say almost all of our politicians that are in public office and are running for public office. Who would I consider a master of psychological warfare? I think Bill Clinton would fall under that definition of mastery. I would also have to say that the Democratic Party, as a whole, is better at psychological warfare than the Republican Party.

Internal Strife

When a country is near its collapse, most of the time internal strife is out of control. I wonder how many people of the Shang Dynasty were killed by the people of the tribe of Zhou because they wanted revenge for the acts of King Di Xin (Zhou). Is this the situation we are having in the inner cities in our country? Have we allowed our federal government to hold these people down with their welfare programs, and other federal government programs, to where these people have lost all hope for a better life?

What's interesting now is the same liberal Democrats that have come up with these federal government programs have their sights on the middle class. They don't want to have a redistribution of wealth from the rich politicians. They want a redistribution of the middle class and rich non-politician wealth. This will establish a society like China.

In China's society, during the end period of a dynasty's timeframe, you had the extremely rich, the rich, the poor and the extremely poor. The middle class of China was wiped out due to the government's levy of taxation. At certain times in China's history, the taxes on the peasants was as high as 60%..

Michael Moore just recently said that we the people of the United States should pay that high of a tax. It's interesting that a man who probably has millions of dollars, who has it invested and lives off the interest, would say such a thing. You see, the rich people in our country have their money invested and live off a portion of that interest. If this interest is not from tax-free bonds or other tax-free exemptions, then they have to pay taxes on this interest and dividends, while we have to pay this tax on our wages. This is one of the reasons the rich get richer and the poor get poorer.

Why did Shang Tang rebel against the Xia Dynasty? If we can trust the historical records of China, then we can see that Shang Tang was a virtuous man who was disgusted by the barbaric treatment of the people. He saw what the heavy tax burden was doing to the people around him and saw the need for change.

It is one thing for a government to levy a fair tax, but to levy taxes to the point where you couldn't feed your family is another. I believe that Barack Obama is going to try this. We will all have to go on food stamps. It is also bad to have taxes so high that you have to work 12-hour days to make ends meet. When governments get to this point and the people find that life isn't worth living, they rebel. Have we reached this point in our country? Not yet, but I believe that the federal government is rapidly bringing on this situation.

It is interesting, however, that the history of the Chinese Dynasties shows that the Shang and the Zhou dynasties overthrew the previous dynasty because of the king's behavior. The last king of the Shang Dynasty was supposedly a tyrant, and the people of that dynasty, during their end days, couldn't feed their families due to the high taxes levied on them.

I do believe the tax part of the history of the Shang Dynasty, but I'm not so sure about the last king being a tyrant. Why believe the tax part? I see that being played out today in the United States. It is interesting, to see throughout history that when a nation is on the verge of collapse, the government of that nation levies a tax burden, on its people, which usually brings on a rebellion. So you can imagine the chaos that must have been going on, in the countryside of the Shang Dynasty.

Do politicians fail to see the writing on the wall? Do they fail to see that their greed for power and wealth is destroying their country? Do politicians believe that their corruption will not cause the fall of their country, in their lifetime?

Why, might I think that ancient Chinese history wouldn't be accurate? As a whole, I think their history is accurate, but I also know that people have emotions and agendas. We can see that being played out today with the rewriting of the Clinton legacy. Will we, ever face the facts that some people will do anything to get a positive written statement of themselves, into the history books? I see history of today being rewritten by special interest groups, in the effort to try to make one of their own look good. I do wonder sometimes how accurate ancient history is when I see this rewrite of history happening in my lifetime. Why do I think this is happening in my lifetime? Well, you see, Bill Clinton is trying to rewrite history and his legacy with his book that he got published. It is 980 torturous pages of his life (lies).

Instead of Bill Clinton telling us that he let us down. That he was too busy to care about the welfare of our country because of his pleasure-seeking attitude. He is trying to get us to believe that he was a president, who should be put up there with the likes of a Ronald Regan, Franklin Delano Roosevelt, John Kennedy or Theodore Roosevelt.

The Zhou Dynasty

The Zhou Dynasty lasted for around 800 years, the longest-lasting dynasty of China. The Zhou Dynasty had four distinctive divisions to its existence. Some historians say there were two different dynasties. The Western Zhou Dynasty and Eastern Zhou Dynasty; the Eastern Zhou Dynasty had two time periods to it. These were "the Spring & Autumn Period and Warring State Period."[7] I just look at it as having four divisions of time within this dynasty's history. The Western Zhou existence is estimated to start at about 1122 B.C. or 1027 B.C. When the barbarians sacked Western Zhou in 771 B.C. and killed King You. The Eastern Zhou came into existence in 770 B.C., when King Ping moved the capital to Luoyi. The Spring & Autumn Period started at 722 B.C. and ended at 481 B.C., and naturally the Warring State Period lasted until 221 B.C. The Spring & Autumn Period "saw a proliferation of new ideas and philosophies."[8]

Out of Spring & Autumn Period, three main philosophies were born: Daoism, Confucianism and Legalism. In the Warring State Period, the larger states were battling with each other for the control of China. In this period, warfare changed. Instead of having small battles that lasted for a day, it changed to armies having 500,000 men and having battles lasting until a victor was established.

Even though we are looking at about 800 years of history and the Zhou Dynasty starting the Mandate of Heaven, it seems that we are seeing a pattern emerging. This pattern seems to be, to get around the possibility that the historical writers of their time, would seriously look down upon the actions, of a conquer conquering the pervious dynasty. So they needed to come up with something that would justify the overthrow of the pervious dynasty. So the Mandate of Heaven was invented.

Each conquer in his time period that overthrew the previous dynasty used the excuse that the king was a tyrant. In the case with the Zhou, they came up with the Mandate of Heaven or the loss of the Mandate of Heaven to rule China. "The only way to know if the Mandate of Heaven had been removed from the ruling family was if they were overthrown."[9] "If the ruler is overthrown, then the victors had the Mandate of Heaven."[10] This sounds a little bit like Daoism.

I see a similar pattern with the liberal Democrats in our country. They try to use the ploy that Reagan, Bush 41 and Bush 43 were and are half-wits or slow, and don't have the intelligence to run our country. Why do liberal Democrats speak like this? Why do they speak from both sides of their mouths? I think that Bill Clinton didn't have the moral clarity to run our country, but I didn't see any liberal Democrats stating that. I really wonder if any of our politicians in Washington, have the moral clarity to run our country. They also say that no one should question their patriotism, for not supporting the war on terrorism, but then turn around and call someone stupid for not having the same ideals as they do.

This has always interested me, how an enemy of the United States can throw out such hatred for our country in a speech, then see liberal Democrats turn around and support that person and expect us not to question their patriotism. This just amazes me

Who was to Blame for the fall of the Western Zhou Dynasty?

Who should have been blamed for the fall of the Western Zhou Dynasty? Some say it was King You, while others say it was his Queen Baosi. A Confucian writer blamed the Western Zhou Dynasty's destruction on King You. King You tried many times to get Baosi to smile. He failed at every attempt. Finally he got her to burst out into laughter when he had the early warning system sounded, which was used to alert the sovereign rulers that an advancing army was coming. King You used the early warning system so much that when the barbarians did attack, no one took the warning seriously, and the barbarian tribes sacked the Western Zhou Dynasty.

"Consequently King You was killed, and Baosi was taken away."[11] King You, who had the early warning system constructed to warn of impending doom, knew that there was a barbarian threat to his kingdom. So why would he use this for his wife's pleasure? He must have known that the early warning system would become useless if used to often. This is another example in history, which shows what happens to your country when you get someone in power, which doesn't care about anybody but himself/herself. When the Twin Towers were attacked in New York City in 1993 and in 2001, were these attacks cause by Bill Clinton's lack of concern for our country? I believe they were.

I like these Chinese idioms: "A single smile costs one thousand pieces of gold" and "The sovereign rulers are fooled by the beacon fire."[12] I believe that this is being played out in our country today. We the people of the United States are so wrapped up in our appetite for amusement that we are fooled by our politicians in Washington.

The Beginning of the Western Zhou Dynasty

How did the Western Zhou Dynasty come about? They were a semi-nomadic tribe that "settled in the area of the Wei River valley where they became vassals of the Shang."[14] Chinese history states that the Zhou where able to overthrow the Shang Dynasty because of three main reasons. The first was that the "Shang had degenerated morally."[15] The second was the Zhou could gain "the allegiance of disaffected cities-states."[16] The third and the most important is they "became stronger than the Shang," due to the Shang having so many wars with the barbarian tribes to the north. [17]

When the Zhou started their dynasty, they moved the Shang communities and families into different parts of the cities they just built, so they could use the knowledge of the Shang. Although they keep some of the Shang culture and lived in the same cities, the Zhou practiced a separate form of lifestyle; the Shang weren't allowed to live in the same area of the city as the Zhou did. I find this to be interesting. The Chinese had prejudices and hatreds as we do today.

How many of you remember the separate but equal treatment of the White and Black populations?

The Zhou started a feudal form of government, which caused them trouble later on, which plagued China with trouble in certain segments of their history. Their form of government reminds me of the government the colonies of the United States formed right after their Revolutionary War. They managed to get rid of the federation style of government before it became too entrenched into our society. The Chinese didn't have enough foresight to see the complication to the feudal style of government.

The feudalism system of the Zhou Dynasty caused them trouble, due in part to the weakness of the central government. Regional strongmen eventually realized that they didn't have to obey the edicts of the king's central government and could control their area of influence themselves. Some of these regional strongmen rebelled against the king and formed an alliance with the barbarian tribes of the south. Do we have a warlord system in our country? Yes, we have something like that, although we call them gangs and organized crime.

The Turbulent Years of China: Have They Been Transferred To the United States?

Chapter 12

The turbulent years of China started after the White Lotus rebellion was put down by the Qing Dynasty. Historians might argue about this by saying that China has had many turbulent periods in their 5,000 years of existence, which is true. But the Warring State Period and the Three Kingdom Period were nothing in comparison to what the Chinese went through during the end period of the Qing Dynasty.

The Manchurians started to lose control of China after the Chinese people saw their failure to quickly crash the White Lotus Rebellion. This set the groundwork for the oppressed to start pushing back against the oppressors.

The Qing Dynasty was plagued with rebellions, western power intrusions and an illegal drug problem that got out of control during the 19th and 20th centuries. It is estimated that 50 million Chinese lost their lives during this timeframe. I would call that turbulent.

Now the question is, how have the turbulent years of China been transferred to the United States? The United States has an illegal drug problem that matches if not exceeds China's, in the 19th century. We haven't had open rebellion yet, but from what I'm seeing from our economy, I wouldn't be surprised if we don't have street demonstrations, which will make the 1960s look tame. This is it, only these two things and I think that we are having turbulent years in the United States.

The turbulent years of China didn't start overnight, and I don't believe that the Chinese people thought that they were living in turbulent years. Where the Chinese turbulent years started, will be debated for a long period of time. Our turbulent years started back in the 1930s with the Great Depression. I relate the Great Depression to the White Lotus rebellion of China. Yes, we got out of the Great Depression and life went on. WWII started and the people working in the military industry were leading prosperous lives, even though we had men fighting and dying over in Europe and Asia.

Then the Korean War hit, and once again we were fighting in Asia. We got out of that pretty well, mostly unmolested. The Vietnam War started and we went to war again. The Vietnam War started our energy crisis in the 1970s, which we haven't recovered from. Now we have a war on terrorism, a war on drugs, and an illegal immigration problem.

The wars on terror, if we decide to turn our tails and run back home, won't be like the Korean War or like the Vietnam War. The terrorists will follow us back home, and instead of fighting on their soil we will be fighting on our soil, and the population of this country might begin to understand what terrorism is all about. We then can thank the Democratic Party for their naiveté. We could even see the loss of life that China saw in the Taiping Rebellion, which was 20 million to 30 million people.

The war on drugs, we are losing. This reminds me of the drug problem China was faced with, where foreign countries such as Great Britain smuggled in drugs to gain a balance in trade. Great Britain actually went to war to force China to accept this trade, forget that this was devastating to the Chinese people and their country. A profit to England must be made, no matter what the cost to other nations or people.

We have the drug cartels smuggling in drugs for profit and in the process, the drug users become drug addicts. This hurts the economy of any country through lost jobs, health and rehabilitation care. The drug cartels haven't threatened us with a war to keep their drugs flowing into our country, but I kind of wonder if they really need to. All of our efforts to stop the drug flow have failed.

I'm at odds with myself with this. At first I didn't think that China had an illegal immigration problem, as we have today. Then I start to think about the foreign countries forcing their way into China and forcing a so-called free trade agreement upon them. With these foreign powers came people, which I believe the Chinese government didn't want in their country. So when the Chinese government demanded that these people obey Chinese law, they just basically laughed at the Chinese and did what they wanted. Just like the illegal immigrants that come into our country on a daily basis, and basically doing whatever they want.

This so-called free trade agreement actually brought China down to a semi-colonial power 50 to 60 years later. China didn't want this so-called free trade agreement, but what a sovereign nation wants doesn't matter when it comes to economic power, and money.

What are some of the ramifications of illegal immigration? The one ramification that everyone needs to worry about is this: Do we have the jobs here to employ these people? Countries set up immigration laws for reasons, which most people don't even think about. The main reason for immigration laws is to ensure that these people, who want to emigrate from their country to our country, have the potential to find work.

If we let one segment of a society into our country and don't have the necessary work available for them, what happens? Since we all need to eat, and since it takes money to buy food, what will these people do for money? They will turn into criminals and use crime as a means to get money to buy food. Some will turn to crime whether we have the jobs available or not. I hope the people of the United States are ready for this.

Now these émigrés who come to our country for criminal activities will either engage in uneducated crime or educated crime. The ones that participate in uneducated crime will get caught, and go to jail for those activities, at our expense. The ones that engage in educated crime have a better chance of getting away with it. It's hard to get evidence on these people because they set up an organization, and usually give orders to their staff, to carry out these criminal activities.

The Events in China that Led to the fall of the Qing Dynasty

So the events that led up to the fall of the Manchurian Dynasty (Qing Dynasty), are they happening in our country now? When the Qing Dynasty fell, the dynasty era in China was over. The Qing Dynasty was the last of the true dynasties.

China's turbulent years deepened in the last days of the Qing Dynasty, due in part to the weakness of the centralized government and in part to the western powers, along with Japan, which were carving up China like a melon. When the Qing Dynasty fell, China went from turbulent years to years of chaos. The main reason for the fall of China's last dynasty was from the foreign powers' greed. With greed, corruption comes.

The foreign powers each wanted some of China's economic strength through trade treaties, and in the process of forcing China into these trade dealings, they brought on the collapse of China's national government and put her into the status of a semi-colonial power. The foreign powers were involved in taking away China's sovereignty. Historians say that this started with Great Britain after the opium wars; the nations that came after Great Britain were France, Italy, Germany, Russia, Japan and the United States. Each one of these nations, except for the United States, set up a sphere of influence for them to operate in, but they all wanted a piece of the economic pie of China.

"The United States enunciated the Open Door policy for China; it sought only the preservation of equal opportunity for ordinary trade within the spheres, not the destruction of the spheres themselves."[1] These spheres of influence that were carved out by the European countries and Japan, took away China's sovereignty. It also helped, to usher in a warlord system with regional strongmen battling for territory and power.

This sort of reminded me of the Warring State Period in China's history. The Warring State Period took place under the Eastern Zhou dynasty. There were turbulent wars between the remaining seven states, until the Qin Kingdom defeated the other kingdoms and united China under one emperor. The difference between these two periods in China's history is that during the Warring State Period, there wasn't massive chaos. There were seven kingdoms, which had a government in place for their people.

This also reminds me of today, where the United Nation is trying to take away the sovereignty of the United States by having France call for the people of the United States to pay a 1% world tax. I wonder if Barack Obama is going to go along with such ridiculous nonsense. I know Bill Clinton would have. Time will tell with Barack Obama. The question we should be asking is: Are we the people of the United States willing to tolerate this kind of foreign aggression on our country? As long as it's just talk, we probably will, but if the United Nations tries to levy a world tax on us. We should demand that our federal government take immediate action to stop such a tax.

Now the Chinese government had no choice but to accept whatever the foreign powers wanted, due to the weakness of the Chinese military, which was brought on by the rebellions of the 19th century, along with the wars with Great Britain and France. China fought at least three wars with these two nations. The first opium war was against Great Britain alone, over opium smuggling. "The second opium war followed with Great Britain and France in alliance against China."[2] The war with France was over Vietnam.

The foreigners in China were not held to the laws of China. This into itself shows the blatant disregard for China's sovereignty. When the foreigners broke the law, they were put on trial by their own countrymen and were subjected to the laws of their own country. They were usually let go under some technicality.

This is happening in Great Britain today with their Muslim population. The Muslims are showing a blatant disregard for Britain's sovereignty. The Muslims want to be held accountable to their own form of justice, which is Sharia law. The Muslims want their own form of laws to be accepted by the government of Great Britain, and instead of being tried in a British court of law. They want to be tried in a Sharia court of law. They want to be tried under their original country's laws. Could this be an attempt to get away with what they have done, because under their laws what they have done might not be consider a crime?

This also sounds a lot like our justice system we have today. We have judges passing laws by legislating from the bench. They're ignoring our Constitution when it applies to them. They usually will find a way of letting off their cronies whenever possible. Some of these judges even say that they are following the Constitution, but when they are questioned, where does it says that in our Constitution, they say it is to their interpretation. I might give them that, but when they quote foreign laws to back up their decision on a ruling, then we the people of the United States should demand that our Congress take action. They are the legislative branch of our government, not the judicial branch.

Our laws are based on our Constitution, not foreign laws. The only time foreign law can be used is when an international treaty has been signed by us, the United States, which means that it becomes part of our Constitution, or at least that's the way I understand it.

Now back to the warlords. Although the warlords in China held land and power in their region, their power didn't extend into the major city areas, which were controlled by the foreign powers. The greed that these foreign powers had for money and power was China's downfall, and is probably why we have trouble today getting free trade agreements with China.

The people of China during this time had to deal with the troubles of a bad economy, a warlord system and the foreign powers establishing spheres of influence in their country. The main trouble the Chinese people had was being put in the middle between the foreign powers and the warlords. I have seen this same situation in the inner cities of the United States. Poor people are put between the police and gang members.

Our main trouble that we have to deal with today, in our society is with liberal Democrats. They want to give our sovereignty to the United Nations and put us into a semi-colonial situation that China was in. We are also stuck in the middle, between the liberal Democrats and the conservatives. The liberal Democrats want to take away our freedoms and put us into a socialistic society. While the conservatives want to maintain our freedoms and let us keep some of our earnings.

In the middle of the 19th century, China lost her sovereignty as a nation. Due to the intrusion by the western powers and Japan, China was plunged into chaos. Seeing this, why would anyone in their right mind want to give their sovereignty away? This leads me to ask these questions: Why do liberal politicians want to make us a semi-colonial power to the United Nations? Why do they want to give away our sovereignty to the U.N.? I believe I can answer these questions. One is probably because they feel guilty for the wealth they have, and want us to pay for their feelings of guilt. Usually people who feel guilty about their wealth are the people who got it through illegal activities. Another reason might be that they feel that they can control the U.N. and increase their sphere of influence. They could also have a mental disorder, as Michael Savage thinks, or have a lifestyle where they need more money to support it. The only place left to get this money is from our military budget, which will weaken our national security. Therefore we would need to find someone to protect us. They probably believe that being put under U.N. control will protect us from our lack of military spending.

I truly believe these liberal Democrats want to lay down the foundation for a one-world government, which will be run by one man. The Bible talks about this in the book of Revelation. So should we rename the Democratic Party after the rock band KISS? I think that the Democratic Party really should be called KISS (Knights in Satan's Service). These liberal Democrats might not know that they are doing Satan's will, but if you believe the Bible is the word of God and that God has spelled this out in the book of Revelation, then who do you think will run the one world government?

Do liberal politicians and liberal organizations have our best interest at heart, or are they right now undermining our national security, so the one-world government can be set up? For a one-world government to happen, something has to happen to the United States as a world power. What better way of weakening us than to put us under the control of the United Nations, and ask them for permission to defend ourselves or for them to defend us? Another way is to do what Barack Obama is doing. If he can bankrupt us as a nation, then the United Nations will have little opposition for world domination.

What these liberal politicians and liberal organizations are saying about being put under the control of the U.N. sounds good. They say that we should be held accountable to the world as a superpower, and we have an obligation to the world as the only superpower left. Therefore let's be held accountable to the United Nations. They also give out a spiel about spending less money on our military if we would go this route.

Then we could divert this money for needed social programs, so more people can be taken care of by the hard-working citizens of the United States. This does sound good to those who want to be taken care of. In reality, someone else has to pay for someone to be taken care of. What these people don't understand is that they are losing their freedoms while someone else is having their earnings confiscated.

If we gave up our sovereignty, we wouldn't have to be the policemen of the world but in reality we would be spending more money on the United Nations' military than if we just kept ours. Since we have the most powerful military on the face of the earth, the United Nations would want to join our military with theirs, so more of our young men and women would be in harm's way. Then the United Nations would become the policemen of the world.

One other thing to think about: Would the United Nations' leadership be as forthcoming with information about our young men and women, fighting in certain regions of the world as our own federal government would be? Think twice before you throw our sovereignty away. Think twice before we see our young men and women being put under the leadership of a foreign dictator.

Could I be wrong about these liberal Democrats? Yes, that's possible, but to be a servant of the one-world order, you have to have a negative outlook on life and liberal Democrats truly have that. Look at what liberal Democrats hate: they hate change, competition, honesty, the military, independent people, self-achievement, morals, responsibility and discipline.

China in the Past Hated Tax Cuts, Liberals Hate Tax Cuts Today

The Chinese government never reduced the burden of taxes on their citizenry until the Qing Dynasty. The Qing Dynasty in their prosperous years actually reduced the taxes on the peasantry. Until the Qing Dynasty, the only way the Chinese people got any kind of tax relief was to have a successful rebellion and form a new dynasty. China's current government must have learned from the past, because the average citizen right now in China doesn't pay any tax. So why haven't the liberal Democrats learned that we the citizens of the United States, are getting tired of paying high taxes? Will liberal Democrats ever learn that their failed social programs are killing our nation?

The reason liberal politicians will never learn is because they will not take any information or advice from inferior beings, such as the citizenry of the United States, the working class people. The only way that liberal politicians will learn, is if we keep them out of power for a long period of time by voting in third party candidates. Then they might realize who gives them the power to rule. If you haven't got it by now, either you are blind or naïve. If you truly look at what liberal politicians and liberal organizations have done and are doing, then you should know that they only care about themselves and power.

The failed social programs of liberal Democrats have destroyed our families and are in the process of destroying our nation. So why can't we change the failed policies of liberal Democrats? Liberals hate change. They don't want to change anything, because they're afraid that it might make them look bad. So they would rather see the people or the country suffer, then for them to change a failed policy.

Liberals love high taxes and really get upset when someone proposes tax cuts across the board, which would favor the middle class. Despite what they say about only raising taxes on 5% of the population, this tax that Barack Obama is proposing is going to reach every working man/woman in the United States. This will be mostly through job loss.

We really should know better. If the liberal Democrats could take all the money away from the rich, they would get about $1 trillion. This would give them less than a third of the yearly federal government's budget. Then the question is: Where would they get money after that? If they only increased the taxes on dividends of the super-rich, the tax money, the federal government would get would be about $100 billion; a drop in the bucket, as they would say.

Tax cuts in general anger liberal politicians. John Kerry wants to raise the gasoline tax by 50 cents per gallon and repeal the George Bush tax cuts. I know the lie, his party is trying to push over on the people of the United States. It goes something like this: George Bush's tax cut only benefited the super-rich, which is only one percent of the population. Refer to chapter 3. If George Bush's tax cuts only benefited the super-rich, then how did the economy become so stimulated? If the economy rebounded to where unemployment was only 4.5 % in 2006, with only 1% of the population getting a tax cut, imagine what it would do, if the liberal Democrats would allow the middle class a tax cut? Despite what the liberals are telling you, they fought hard to make sure no one got a tax cut. What they were truly trying to do was to increase taxes at all levels but theirs.

You see, liberal Democrats believe that Clinton's tax increases caused the economy boom of the mid to late 1990s, but in reality his tax increase did nothing but hurt the economy. The dot.com scam is what stimulated the economy until it went bust. After the eight years of Clinton, George Bush inherited an economy that was in recession. Now Barack Obama has inherited an economy that is in recession. What is Barack Obama's answer to our problems? Raise taxes, increase government intervention in our free markets and use taxpayers' money for bailouts. I don't believe this will work. Taking disposable income from the people of the United States will only intensify the recession.

Why do liberal Democrats love high taxes? I believe it is based on their belief system. You see, I'm basing this on my belief system, which is Christianity. When you become a Christian, you believe that God created everything through Jesus Christ. If you believe this, then everything belongs to Jesus. The difference between Jesus and liberal Democrats is that Jesus promised you an abundant life if you believe in him. Liberal politicians believe that their government should receive the abundance of your labors.

Jesus said: The more you can manage, the more I will give you. Liberals say: The more you make, except for me, the more the government should take. Sounds like communism to me. At best it's socialism. Than liberal politicians say that they will decide what this money should be spent on, which is more failed social programs.

Liberal politicians believe that the federal government is god and that everything belongs to the government. We should feel honored that liberal politicians want to use us as a tax base, and if you have to work until June every year to pay for their social programs, well you'll just have to get over it. I believe this is why, they can't understand why anyone would want a tax cut. Just believe in their god (the government) and everything will be okay. You will be given a meager existence, which should be enough.

I wonder if a Ted Kennedy and a John Kerry, when they're in the Senate at the podium and they start their spiel about raising our taxes, if they don't start to drool like a dog, hungry for a steak. I wonder if they start thinking about how much money they can get for their god, by screwing over the wage earners who pay taxes in the United States. I wonder if they think by raising taxes, they can manage to force other people down, so they can maneuver them into a new voting base for their liberal agenda.

Liberals Hate Competition

Why have a section on liberal politicians' hatred for competition in this chapter. It's like this: If you refuse to compete, then you will be left behind, wondering what happened to you. This will cause internal strife among the people of the United States, which will add to the turbulence in our society. So why do they hate competition? We as responsible adults have to compete on a daily basis. When we are young, we compete in many ways; sports for one, grades in our government-run schools and for our mate when we get older and want to start a family. Competition paved the way for us when we became adults. What do we compete in as adults, other than for our mate? The most obvious is work. We have to have a job to get money to support our families and ourselves.

If you are not taught how to compete, then you will need government assistance in your life, and I believe this is what liberals hope for. They believe that if they can get you on the public dole of the federal government, they will have a voter for life. It doesn't matter to them, if you are suffering or your family is suffering, as long as you are part of their voting base. This has worked for them from the 1960s to the 2000s.

One example of the hatred for competition is the school vouchering system. The school vouchering program would put competition back into our schools, by letting the parents decide where their children would get the best education. Barack Obama and Congress have put a stop to the school vouchering system; well, at least in the Washington, D.C. area. So why do liberal politicians think that the school vouchering system is a bad idea?

They don't say it is a bad idea, they come up with some bogus argument that other children will lose out, if money is diverted from the government-run school system to the privately-run school system. This has nothing to do with children losing out; it has everything to do with the teachers' union and their unwillingness to compete for the students. So the teachers' union wants a monopoly on education.

I thought liberal politicians were the compassionate ones. I thought they were the ones who cared. I thought they cared about the children. What they truly are is the party who wants power at any cost, and in this case, it's our children that are paying the price.

The Semi-Colonial Years, Which Brought Chaos to China

During the beginning of the 20th century in China, two men had different ideas on how China should be led into the future. These men were in the political arena, which reminds me of our situation we are having with Liberals and conservatives. One of these men was Yuan Shikai, the other was Song Jiaoren. Yuan Shikai was fighting to become emperor of China, while Song Jiaoren was fighting to bring a parliamentary-style government to China.

Yuan Shikai ordered the assassination of Song Jiaoren, and in March of 1913 Song was murdered. With the believed threat to Yuan Shikai eliminated, he then thought everything would fall into place for him. He didn't realize that there were other people that opposed him. These threats to his power were never eliminated, so Yuan Shikai didn't come up with the desired result to his plan.

When Yuan Shikai declared himself Emperor, he had to relinquish that declaration. He had too much armed opposition to his claim. Even though Yuan Shikai's plans of being emperor of China failed, he became the first dictator of China, or at least the dictator to the part of China he had control over.

It would have been interesting to see what China would have been like if Song Jiaoren would have succeed. Song Jiaoren was the architect of the constitution and the leader of the Nationalist Party (Guomindang Party).

Yuan Shikai thought if he killed off the leader of the majority party (Nationalist Party) the minority party leaders would fall in line with him. Well, he was wrong. He still might have gotten what he wanted, but he missed his golden opportunity when he failed to harness the Nationalist Party's cause to his own. Instead, he forced a showdown with the Nationalist Party by forcing their governors out of office. Naturally, this started a revolution. This revolution is referred to by some historians as the Second Revolution. Yuan Shikai defeated these insurgents easily, and in this uprising Sun Yat-sen was forced into exile and went to Japan.

Sun Yat-sen was a member of the Nationalist Party of China. While in exile in Japan, he tried to get support from the Japanese for his cause. He came back to China after Yuan Shikai died in 1916, and tried to reform the Nationalist Party into a viable organization. His attempts failed. He then tried to strengthen the party by forming an alliance with the Chinese Communist Party (CCP). Sun Yat-sen's alliance with the CCP reminds me of the alliance the Black organizations have made with the Democratic Party in the United States.

This alliance between the CCP and the Nationalists at first seemed to have benefits for both parties. But the CCP was forced out in 1928, when Chiang Kai-shek brought back a national government to China. It's interesting to see throughout history the efforts organizations will make to obtain power. Chiang Kai-shek became the second dictator of China after the death of Sun Yat-sen in 1925. Chiang Kai-shek started his dictatorship in 1926.

Although the Blacks were not kicked out of the Democratic Party, I believe, you can see the same effects of the alliance between the Black organizations and the Democratic Party. Both organizations benefited at first, or at least it seems that way. The Black organizations of the United States got Affirmative Action for their people. They got a quota system implemented for the young men and women, to receive special treatment when it comes to college exams, jobs, welfare and other opportunities in the United States. They have received this special treatment for over 40 years. Has this special treatment helped the Black race, or has this special treatment held the Black people back? I believe it has held them back. The Black population in our country is still at the bottom rung of the economic ladder.

Affirmative Action handled correctly would have been a good federal government program, for the minorities in the United States. The way Affirmative Action should have been used was when true discrimination was being practiced. True discrimination practices would have been obvious to see. This would show true discrimination, when a minority was denied entry into college, when they were in the top ten percent of the S.A.T. test scores. Instead, what Affirmative Action did was to guarantee a percentage of minorities an entry into colleges across the United States. Why is this bad? When you don't have to work to get anything, you become lazy. Ask anyone who has been on unemployment. When everything is handed to you, do you really appreciate it? I don't believe you can appreciate anything unless you earn it and understand what it took, to get it or to achieve it.

Sun Yat-sen had a Different Idea of a Government for China than What Occurred

Sun Yat-sen had a different idea of a government for China than a dictatorship. Sun Yat-sen wanted a five-branch government. Three branches of his government would have been like ours, with an addition of two more branches, which would have controlled the corruption and would have tested the intelligence of the politicians running for public office.

The branch of government that would have tried to control corrupt politicians in Sun Yat-sen's government is interesting, to say the least. Did Sun Yat-sen look through the history of China and see that the reason China's dynasties fell, was because of the corrupt bureaucrats? Did he want to try to protect his government from such corruption?

It seems that these bureaucrats in China's past had life-long positions given to them by the emperor, and after a taste of wealth and power, they would do anything to increase their prestige. This included the undermining of their country's security; something liberal politicians are doing right now in the attempt to keep power.

Sun's other branch of government, which would have tested the intelligence of the politicians running for public office. This is probably a throwback to the old imperial days. The people who wanted to be the bureaucrats (gentries) had to pass a series of tests to get their position in government. This became corrupted, too. It seems that people will become corrupt, whenever there is power to be had. The one thing that might have stopped the corruption, in this branch of government, which would have tested the bureaucrat's Intelligence, was the branch of government that was set up to stop corruption. Do I think that the one branch of government, which was set up to stop corruption in the other four branches of government, would not have become corrupt? I believe that it would have become corrupt because it would be run by power hungry men. So it might not have worked, but it would have been interesting to see how this type of government would have done.

Should we add these branches to our government, to control corruption and test the intelligence of our politicians? We supposedly have a government department that is to control corruption and it's doing a very poor job. This department is controlled by our elected officials. In other words, they are policing themselves. I think we need to add two branches to our government that will control corruption and test the intelligence of our politicians. Although we might have trouble finding people with the intelligence needed to hold public office, I still think we should do it.

I believe an example of politicians not having the intelligence to run for public office would be these three: Ted Kennedy, John Kerry and John McCain. These three have trouble grasping the importance of being a public servant. We'll see if Barack Obama understands the meaning of public servant. I personally believe he won't, but we will see one way or another.

So what happened to Sun Yat-sen's idea? Why didn't Sun Yat-sen get his way? "Inoperable liver cancer" took Sun Yat-sen. He died in March of 1925. [3] "After the death of Sun Yat-sen, Chiang Kai-shek became the leader of the Kuomintang army and seized control of the government". [4] Chiang Kai-shek became the new leader of the Nationalist Party (Guomindang or Kuomintang Party). He decided to declare martial law in March of 1926. Chiang Kai-shek didn't have an easy time as the dictator of China. He had to deal with the Japanese invasion of Manchuria, and before that the CCP was waging guerrilla warfare against him.

Although Chiang Kai-shek was having a difficult time maintaining his control of China, he held on to power until 1949. Why did he last so long? World War II broke out, and with the Japanese invasion of Manchuria, the CCP and the Nationalist Part once again joined forces to eliminate the Japanese threat.

Some historians say that WWII gave Chiang Kai-shek a reprieve until 1949, while others say that WWII gave the CCP a reprieve. I believe that WWII gave the CCP the reprieve. It gave them the time needed, to recruit people and to refine and train their people in the art of guerrilla warfare. The CCP also recruited people who would be willing to fight and die for their cause.

Currently, the Democratic Party in the United States is like the CCP in China, in the 1930s and 1940s. The Democrats will lie, cheat, steal, deceive, connive, tell half-truths, and make you think that they are for the middle class of the United States. This is the furthest thing from their minds. Democrats only care about power. They only care about maintaining their power and growing the federal government, and will do anything to obtain it.

Is the semi-colonial era of China a prelude for us, will we allow our country to become a semi-colonial power under the control of the United Nations?

Why Did the Nationalists Lose?

The Nationalists took power in 1928 under the leadership of Chiang Kai-shek. The country of China had a new national government. They seemed to make the same mistake all the governments before them did. They forgot about the welfare of the peasantry. This alone helped the CCP.

The Nationalist government didn't even think an education system should be brought down to the level of the peasantry, in their society. This was left to the CCP, which in return got them the support they needed from the peasants. What the Nationalist Party of China should have done is what the Democratic Party has done in our country, which is to come up with a government-run school system that doesn't educate the children. It makes them look like they care when they truly do not. This type of deceitful conniving deception seems to have worked quite marvelously for the Democratic Party.

I have pondered this for quite some time. Which is worse? A government or a political party that doesn't care about their people and makes no bones about it, or a political party that seems to care for the people, but the results of their actions show otherwise? Chiang Kai-shek apparently didn't care for the welfare of the peasants and made no excuses for it. While in our country, we have the Democratic Party of Ted Kennedy, John Kerry and Bill Clinton, who say they care about the poor. The only thing that I have seen the Democratic Party do, for the poor was to make them a voting base or give them federal government assistances. This has made them addicted to these programs. To me, false caring is worse than telling someone that you don't care.

The Nationalists had twice the manpower and equipment as the Communists, but lost the war. How did the Communist Party of China defeat the Nationalist Party of China?

It is interesting. At first glance you would think that a better-equipped army would win. The main reason the Communists won was because they were united. They were focused on their goal. They had the backing from a majority of the people of China. The Nationalists weren't focused they were too busy fighting over petty differences, instead of caring about the goal of surviving as a government. Plus they treated the peasants as enemies. This split their country into two different camps; one for the CCP and the other for the Nationalists. The government of a divided nation will not survive. How long does the United States have? That's a good question. I would think 30 years max.

For the Nationalists Party to have survived, they needed to put away their differences until they won the war. Chiang Kai-shek had too many commanders who refused to cooperate with each other. Chiang Kai-shek also refused to let his commanders make decisions in the field of battle. This seems to be a common mistake with leaders who micro-manage. LBJ didn't let his commanders make decisions on the battlefield in Vietnam. He made all the decisions in Washington. This is why the Vietnam War couldn't have been won under his presidency. This also reminds me of liberal politicians. They refused to cooperate with the conservatives on the war against terrorism.

Why did These Two Chinese Dynasties Fall?

Chapter 13

The Qing Dynasty

The Qing Dynasty was entrenched with internal strife that kept them from protecting their country from outside forces; their internal strife caused them to fall apart from within. Does this sound familiar? We are falling apart from within, due to our differences in our ideologies and by allowing political correctness to become a fanaticism in our country.

The Qing Dynasty's internal strife made it difficult for them to protect their country from foreign aggressors. They had to split their resources to suppress rebellions and to try to stop foreign aggressions. The people of the United States should look at the Qing Dynasty if they want to see what awaits us. We are entrenched with political correctness; we refuse to protect our borders and keep out people who want to enter into our country illegally.

As the Qing Dynasty was suffering from open rebellion, our internal strife is a little bit different. We are not in open rebellion against our federal government, but I believe it will come. The producers will get tired of having their taxes raised, to the point where they fall from the status of the middle class. So the non-producers can be taken care of.

When this open rebellion comes to the United States, it will start by states wanting to secede from the union. Then we will see if our federal government looks upon this as a rebellion or as a state's right. I believe that the federal government of the United States will look upon these secessions as open rebellion. Why's that? Isn't it in our Constitution that states may leave the Union? The only reason that the United States government will look upon these secessions as rebellion is because of the loss of tax revenue. The worship of money is the root cause of all evil. Although I don't think the United States government worships money, they will see this revenue lose as money they will not be able to spend, on their beloved social programs.

In China's 5,000 years of history, China has had 24 successful rebellions. The last successful rebellion ushered in the Communist government of China. China has had numerous failed rebellions. The two most famous failed rebellions during the Qing Dynasty were the Taiping Rebellion and the White Lotus Rebellion.

Why are these rebellions the most famous rebellions? Some historians will argue that they are not. The reason I believe they are is because the White Lotus Rebellion shattered "the myth of the Manchurian army's invincibility, while the Taiping Rebellion tried for twenty years, to remove the Manchurians from power."[1] Did our loss of the Vietnam War shatter the myth of our military invincibility?

When the White Lotus Rebellion shattered the myth of the Manchurian army's invincibility, it gave the people oppressed by the Manchurians, the desire and will to rebel against their oppressors. The White Lotus Rebellion set the groundwork for all the rebellions that plagued the Qing Dynasty during the 19th century. The White Lotus Rebellion started in 1796 and lasted until 1804, when it was finally crushed by the Manchurians. It started out as a tax protest, which developed into a full-blown rebellion.

We are starting to see tax protests in the United States, which are organized under the code-name Tea Party. What rate of taxation will bring these protests to a full-blown rebellion in the United States?

The White Lotus Rebellion was started by impoverished "settlers in the mountainous region that separates Sichuan province;" one of their goals was to bring back the native Chinese Ming Dynasty. [2] Was the tax that was levied on these people, used as an excuse for open rebellion, as we used the taxation that the British levied upon us, as our excuse for our War of Independence?

The Taiping Rebellion was a threat to the government of the Qing Dynasty and the philosophy of Confucianism. It was started by Hong Xiuquan and Yang Xiuqing, who wanted to replace Confucian ideology with Christian ideology.

"Hong was an unorthodox Christian convert who declared himself the new Messiah and younger brother of Jesus Christ."[3] Hong thought that he was put on this earth to remove the Manchurians and the ideology of Confucianism because they were the demons that was plaguing the countryside of China. To remove the Manchurians meant you had to remove the Qing Dynasty. To remove Confucian ideology meant you had to outlaw Confucianism or murder the people practicing it.

I kind of wonder why Hong Xiuquan didn't see the foreign aggressors as demons and want to remove them as well. So naturally, the Taiping Rebellion was a revolt against the Qing Dynasty and the ideology of its time. The Qing Dynasty was the government, the power that implemented the laws, so if you wanted change, then you had to overthrow the ruling power.

The second in command, "Yang Xiuqing was a former salesman of firewood," he acted as if he was the mouthpiece of God. [4] This gave him political power over the people of the region. It seems that it doesn't matter where you look into history, you will find people that will come up with gimmicks to deceive the populous. The last gimmick was used by Barack Obama with his gimmick of hope and change.

The Taiping Rebellion "lasted for twenty years," or did it? It depends on what source you read. [5] If I take this direct quote; "nobody thought Hong's rebellion would last fifteen years." [6] Shows the discrepancy between these two sources. Hong committed suicide in 1864 in the 18th year of the rebellion, or was it the 13th year? Once again, there is a discrepancy along these lines on when the rebellion ended. Some historians say the rebellion lasted until 1866, while others say it lasted until 1864, which is when Hong killed himself. However, it seems all of the sources I have read agree that Hong died in 1864.

Hong and Yang set up their kingdom in Nanking. Hong started out as a student, studying for civil service. He failed this examination many times, probably because he wasn't rich or didn't have a government insider backing him. You especially come to this conclusion, when you understand how the opium addiction affected 90% of the Chinese men, from age 40 and under, along the coastal regions of China. The opium addiction plagued China from the 1820s until now. Although you don't hear about it today, I'm sure that they still have a drug problem.

The opium addiction nearly brought the civil service exams to a halt. So, if the Chinese government was begging for civil servants, why did they deny Hong Xiuquan? Did he really fail the test or was he denied for other reasons? This sounds a lot like the United States. You won't get elected to any office of the federal government unless you have the backing of rich people or you are rich. If you are rich or have the backing of the rich, then you are an insider and will be accepted with open arms. I would think that Barack Obama would by a good example of this. He had the backing of the rich Democrats along with the lackeys of the news media. This made him an insider and gave him the presidency of the United States.

On one occasion while Hong was studying for the civil service exams, he had a vision that he was the second son of God and that Jesus was his older brother. Hong didn't do anything with this vision "until seven years later," when he started studying Christianity under the guidance of "Issachar J. Roberts, a Southern Baptist minister who taught him everything he would know about Christianity."[7] Was this vision brought on by the lack of sleep or maybe by smoking some opium, while he was studying? Anyway, under the influence of this vision, he was able to start a rebellion and have it last for roughly 15 years. Or was it 20 years?

Some historians will argue that there were more than 24 successful rebellions and that the Taiping and White Lotus Rebellions were not the most famous, of the rebellions during the Qing Dynasty. There is one thing about studying history, and that is people will come up with different results in historical matters, which is why you will find numerous books written under the topic of history, but one thing you can't argue about is the facts. There were at least 24 successful rebellions, and of all the failed rebellions, the White Lotus Rebellion and the Taiping Rebellion are noteworthy.

Historians will tell you that the most severe threat to the Qing Dynasty was the opium wars with Great Britain. Although the opium wars were a major threat to China, you have to also understand that a nation cannot be subjugated by another unless it is willing to tolerate their presence.

Was their presence tolerated, due to the internal strife occurring in China, at that time? The leadership of China, did they feel that the internal strife in the country was more of a threat to them than these foreign aggressors? The Chinese loss of the opium wars brought on the Qing Dynasty's eventual collapse, due in part to China's appeasement to Great Britain, France, Italy, Germany, Russia, Japan and the United States, and in part to the rebellions besieging China's countryside.

Will we suffer the Qing Dynasty's fate? Will our appeasement to the rest of the world bring on our collapse? Yes, the appeasement we will give to the rest of the world and the turning of our backs on Israel, along with our lack of desire to defend our borders, will bring on our destruction as a nation. It's only a matter of time. We're starting to see our strength as an economic power slip.

What's interesting about China's appeasement is that when China lost the first opium war to Great Britain, France also saw an economic opportunity for them in China. France set up an alliance with Great Britain when the second opium war broke out. China, in their loss of the second opium war, thought they had no choice but to appease these foreign aggressors.

What the Chinese government should have done was make an alliance with the people in rebellion. They should have tried to get the people of China to realize that these foreign aggressors were a true threat, to their country and needed to be removed. Their only hope of removing these western powers was as a nation united. Once that threat was removed, they could settle their differences on the battlefield, but as with all nations, the true threat to the Chinese people was the complacency and apathy of its politicians in government.

So how did these rebellions in China's countryside aid in the downfall of the Qing Dynasty? Anytime you have your nation, at odds with certain groups of people, you will have internal strife. This internal strife will bring corruption with it.

Politicians, in this case, courtiers, will use this internal strife for their own financial gain or for political power. Any time you have to split your resources to defend against domestic and foreign aggressors, you weaken your ability to defend your nation. So are we splitting our resources between illegal immigrants, freeloaders, and domestic and foreign aggressors? I would have to say yes to the domestic and foreign aggressors. With the illegal immigrants, we just let them come in. Sort of the same apathy the Chinese government showed toward foreign aggressors in their country, we are showing to illegal immigrants.

The apathy we have toward illegal immigrants brings on a different kind of resource expenditures. We are now splitting social programs meant for United States citizens with illegal immigrants. These social programs are our health care system, jobs, Social Security and welfare.

Was the opium war with Great Britain a major threat to the Qing Dynasty? Yes, the loss of the opium wars to Great Britain, an outside aggressor to their country, showed the rest of the world how weak China was militarily. The opium trade got started in China in the 1820s. The British found out that opium was the only product, they could sell in China that would give them a profit. The Chinese government wanted to stop the opium imports from Great Britain, after they saw the affects this drug had on its people. "Ninety percent of Chinese males, under the age of forty in the country's coastal regions" were hooked on opium. [8] The consequences of opium imports brought on a drop in the standard of living, to the Chinese people and reduced their business activities. So naturally the Chinese government wanted to put a stop to this drug addiction.

One way to stop an addiction is to stop the supply of the addictive drug. So the Chinese law enforcement, in this case the Chinese army, confiscated all of the British opium and then destroyed it. To show you how much opium the British had, it took the Chinese 23 days to destroy all of it. Now the British weren't going to take this lying down. So Great Britain declared war on China for destroying their property. The first war lasted for about three years. China was defeated by Great Britain.

So Great Britain was still able to rape China. Great Britain, in a peace treaty, was able to dictate terms to China. Here are a few of the terms, "Britain forced Imperial China to pay them an indemnity of 21 million silver dollars." [9] Great Britain was able to steal land and ports to aid them in their immoral trade policies of smuggling opium, British nationals were given extraterritoriality (exemption from Chinese laws) and Great Britain got favorite nation status.

"The outbreak of fresh hostilities under such circumstances was almost inevitable."[10] France and the United States were able to get additional concessions after the signing of the treaty of Nanking, "including clauses about renegotiation after twelve years."[11] In 1854, more raping of the nation of China occurred. China was forced to open all of her ports to Great Britain and exempt British's goods from all import duties; another term was for China to legalize the importation of opium. The Hostilities, which the opium wars were called, continued off and on until 1860. China lost every one of these conflicts, with the western powers and gave more and more concessions, but one must think about the internal strife going on in China at the time.

If China didn't have the Nian Rebellion in the north and the Taiping Rebellion in the south, would China have fared better than they did against the western powers? I believe they would have. I realize that this is only my belief. I still wonder if China didn't have this internal strife going on, how many armies could have been diverted, to the fight against the western powers instead of crushing rebellions.

One of the conditions of the peace treaty in1842 was for China to allow Christian missionaries into China to proclaim the Christian faith. I wonder if this could be one of the reasons the current Chinese government doesn't allow any religion to be practiced openly. After all, Hong Xiuquan started his rebellion under his philosophy of Christianity.

What is amazing to me is that Great Britain, the United States and France were supposedly Christian nations. Were the people running these countries Christians, or were they Christians in name only? Were they not concerned about their actions toward China, or did profit override all concerns of what they were doing, to the Chinese people. Maybe they didn't care, because in their eyes these people weren't Christians and therefore they could rationalize away their actions.

Great Britain and the United States today have a huge drug problem. Is this problem due to the activities of these two countries 150 years ago? The people who practice Buddhism would call this karma. Christians would quote a passage from the Bible about reaping what you sow.

Merchants from Great Britain and the United States, with the backing of these two countries, disguised their activities by calling themselves tea traders, while actually they were drug traffickers. This also shows that Great Britain and the United States were more interested in profits instead of the well being of people. Anyway, Great Britain's solution to their drug problem was to legalize illegal drug use. The United States' solution was to declare a war on illegal drug use. The United States is losing this war.

The representatives of the western powers in China managed to take away Chinese sovereignty and made China a semi-colonial power as a nation. In today's world events, are we seeing this happening to Great Britain and the United States? Great Britain is becoming a semi-colonial power, by being put under the control of the European Common Market. The liberal politicians in the United States want the United States to become a semi-colonial power under the control of the United Nations.

What's interesting in the United States is how China has managed to flood our markets with their goods. Anytime you go to buy something, out of a department store, you will see "made in China." It is very hard to find anything that says made in the United States. I do find this interesting, how often this Bible verse comes true. The Bible verse is "you will reap what you sow."

The Han Dynasty that Splintered into the Three Kingdoms

The Han Dynasty, by 150 A.D. "was already rotting from within," due to weak emperors and corrupt officials, but the empire lasted for another 70 years, before the last emperor was forced to abdicate. [12]

I would say the turning point in the United States started in the 1960s. We started to rot from within, mainly due to our corrupt politicians and with the start of our moral decline. If our corruption is the same as the Han dynasty's corruption, then we have roughly 70 years before our fall. If I'm correct and we started to rot from within, in the 1960s, then we will fall from power in 2030 A.D. The next question is will we split into three different regions as the Han Dynasty did? Anyway, when we do split into many different nations, will we live in peace or will we have constant warfare among us? Right now, we are engaged in political infighting with each other. Hopefully when we split up into many different nations, the political infighting will stop.

The Han Dynasty, in her last days, splintered into the three kingdoms, ushering in 60 years of constant warfare and disunity. This might be where the Chinese saying got started. This is not a direct quote but it goes something like this; "after great unity brings great disunity."

The three kingdoms are considered to have started after the death of Cao Cao, when his son Cao Pi forced the emperor of the Han Dynasty to abdicate his throne. Although the Three Kingdoms Period is not considered to have started until 220 A.D., fighting started way before then. Cao Cao, the prime minister of the Han Dynasty, is the one who held the power. He used the emperor as a puppet.

I believe this will be our fate within the next 30 years. The splintering of our country will start with the standard of living falling, caused by the legislation that will be passed under the Barack Obama's administration. Hard times will come to the United States; blame will fall on the conservatives. Well, someone has to be blamed. We for some reason refuse to blame the people responsible. Most of the time liberal politicians have caused our problems.

"Igor Panarin has been predicting the U.S. will fall apart in 2010 A.D."[13] Will we split into four different countries by 2010, as the Russian professor Igor Panarin predicts? Although this Russian professor is predicting that the United States will split into four different nations by 2010, this would only be possible, if the Democrats, which are in control of our federal government, get everything they want by the end of 2009. Their legislation will bring another Great Depression upon us. How we react to this crisis will determine if we split up our nation in 2010 or if we survive until 2030. I think we will react to this crisis badly. The people that currently live in the United States aren't accustom to hard times. They are accustom, to being taken care of.

Just before the United States splits into four different nations, you will hear more and more talk about the splitting up of our nation into regions. These regions will be split up by the ideologies of the people. The ideologies of people in this country will intensify the disunity of our nation. I can say that we as a nation never had great unity, except for maybe World War II, but right now, I can say we do have great disunity.

The Han Dynasty lasted for about 400 years. It was actually two separate dynasties: the Western Han Dynasty followed by the Xin Dynasty, and the Eastern Han Dynasty. The Western Han Dynasty started around 206 B.C. and ended in 24 A.D. The last emperor was Liu Ying; he had a country in full rebellion. The Western Han Dynasty started to lose it power in 73 B.C.

Some historians say the Western Han Dynasty started to lose their power, due in part to their changing of their promotion system. They use to promote people based on their abilities. They changed to promoting people based on astronomy and fortune telling, to fill government and advisors positions. This sounds like what is happening in Washington today. People are getting government positions based on friendship and party dealings, instead of promoting people based on their abilities.

When the Western Han Dynasty fell, naturally there was a fight for power. "Wang Mang seized the imperial throne" in 9 A.D. and started the Xin Dynasty. [14] "Wang Mang was a devoted Confucianist"; he started his socialist programs in China by "decreeing a return to the golden times" in China, "when every man had his measure of land to till, land that in principle belonged to the state."[15] "He declared that a family of less than eight that had more than fifteen acres was obligated to distribute the excess amount of land to those who had none."[16]

This reminds me of Barack Obama's policies of redistribution of wealth. The only different is land verses money. Wang Mang's socialistic policies didn't work and Barack Obama's socialistic policies won't work. Socialism has never worked, so I don't know why we keep trying to make it work.

Wang Mang also wanted to implement an economic stimulus package by devising a new loan system for the peasantry. "Instead of paying the thirty percent interest that private loaners demanded, Wang Mang offered loans, to those in need, with only ten percent interest."[17] I think that both these policies did him in. He set the peasants and the rich against him.

The peasants didn't want to give up their land and the rich didn't want to earn less money, on their loans to the peasants. So the rich didn't give out loans to the peasants. The peasants didn't have money to work their land and the poor were forced to give up land. This naturally angered the peasants, so they revolted against his policies, and in 25 A.D., the Eastern Han Dynasty was formed and lasted until 220 A.D.

The Three Kingdoms

The Three Kingdoms of China is probably the most famous of China's periods of separation. China has had at least four periods of separation as a nation, but there was always someone who would come up through the ranks and through bloody warfare, would reunite China into one nation. When we split into different nations, will we have someone come up through the ranks to reunite us?

At first, I believe we will try to live and let live, but I think after a certain amount of time we will go into bloody warfare. I believe this because you will always have people that will always want what you have worked hard for.

Yes, we have had one period of separation so far. I consider the seceding of the Southern States a period of separation. This try for separation by the Southern States brought on the Civil War, and after four years of bloody warfare, the United States became one nation again.

So what will bring on the second separation of our country? The political boundaries have been drawn, and from these boundaries two ideologies have emerged; one being immoral, based on liberalism, with the other being moral, based on Christianity. The liberals have declared war on the conservative Christians. A liberal's lifestyle is more important than the security and welfare of the United States.

Should We Use the fall of Rome as a Guide to Ours?

Chapter 14

The Roman Empire has filled volumes of books, had countless documentaries about their rise and fall from world power. What's interesting is how they fell. Were the Roman people just tired of fighting? I wonder if they had the attitude our liberal Democrats have today, which is that everyone else should sacrifice except them.

Will we fill volumes of books and have numerous documentaries about our rise and fall from world power? I believe we will, providing that there's a world interested in doing so after our fall. We are starting to see the documentaries about how our country was formed. If there are historians out there who care, then there will be numerous documentaries on how we fell from world power?

There are countless explanations for why Rome fell from power and why they couldn't protect their land in their latter days, but Rome fell because of their corruption. Our fall will be from our corruption. Their corruption could be different from ours, but corruption gets every nation. The United States is next in a long line of superpowers to fall from world power.

This will make some happy and some sad. The ones who want to form a one-world government will be happy. The ones who want to be free and have their nation retain their sovereignty will be sad. I will be one of the sad ones. I wanted the United States to keep its sovereignty. I would like to see the freedoms restored that we had back in the 1950s, with little if any federal government intrusion and the smallest amount of taxes possible. In other words, I would like to see the people of the United States have the freedoms the Chinese people have.

Rome's corruption came from her politicians. Her politicians did anything and everything they could to keep power, except for keeping their military strong. You would think that these politicians would have realized that they needed a strong military, to protect their borders to stay in power, but then I see our liberal politicians, in our country, who do anything and everything to stay in power except for keeping our military strong. Then I understand why it's not done.

Democrats are notorious for cutting military spending. They then take the money that is saved from cutting military spending and divert it to social program spending. In the process of doing this, they reduce our capability to protect our country, our readiness to protect our people. All one has to do, to see if we were ready for military action, is to look at the Clinton years and see that his military budget cuts were devastating to our country's military readiness.

I believe that this falls under the attitude of "let everyone else sacrifice except me." How's that? People who go into the military sacrifice for the good of the country, while liberal Democrats believe that everyone must sacrifice for them and their special interest groups. Eventually this type of attitude reaches everybody, especially when these people who do sacrifice see people like liberal Democrats not sacrificing. They start to wonder: Why should I have to sacrifice, if this person over here is not sacrificing? I believe that this is what happened to the people of Rome, and I believe this is what starts the apathy and complacency attitudes.

A strong military is crucial to a superpower existence because everybody in the world wants a piece of their economic pie. Some nations are jealous of another nation's prosperity, and other nations just hate your existence. One other reason for a strong military is to keep unwanted guests out of your country, but the military has to be used on your borders, which is the first line of defense of any nation. A strong military can be used as a deterrent against some nations, who feel they have a right to your resources and wealth, but to be a deterrent your military has to be used on the first infraction that is put upon you. One other reason for a strong military is that the first and most important responsibility for a nation's government is to keep its people safe. Our government has failed us in the past and probably will in the future.

This type of failure usually happens under the liberal Democrats' watch. So we'll just have to wait and see what happens under Barack Obama's watch. I hope our death toll is not too high. I get a little worried when I see a person like Barack Obama acting like the Neville Chamberlain of our time, expecting dictators and tyrants to behave themselves.

The Romans' apathy and complacent lifestyle made them fat, dumb, and lazy. Their lifestyle was more important than their country's defense. Today we the citizens of the United States are suffering from that. Have we seen any liberal politician state that we need a strong military to protect our borders from foreign terrorism? I haven't. All I hear from liberal politicians is that we were at fault for being attacked on 9/11/2001, and that we need to become more appeasing to the world, so we are not attacked again. We must find out why they hate us.

You cannot make people like you, and finding out why they hate us will not give us the ability to stop their hatred. Their hatred is from extreme ideology. They don't like our freedom, our lifestyle, or our economic power. So to get them to stop hating us, we would have to live like them. I personally want to live my Christian life in peace. That means I want to be left alone and worship as I see fit, not being forced to praise someone else's god.

We and our children are suffering from apathy and a complacent lifestyle, which is making us fat, dumb, and lazy. Our children do not apply themselves in school. If someone does apply themselves in school, they are made fun of, are called geeks, and in some cases beaten up. The elected liberal representatives and some judges, in their infinite superior wisdom, are trying to stop home schooling, to make sure that these children receive the same poor education as others do.

"Judge Ned Mangum of Wake Country, N.C., ordered devout Christian Venessa Mills to stop home schooling her kids and send them to the government-run Raleigh public school system."[1] I could see this, if the children were being poorly educated, but the judge had to "disregard the fact that the Mills kids have tested two grade levels above their public school peers."[2] This is a good "example of how modern secular elites continually erode individual liberty."[3] I do believe that it would be hard to find "a more basic and intimate sphere of liberty than deciding how one's children will be raised and educated."[4]

So the question that needs to be asked is: Why do parents choose to home school their children? One reason is they can't afford private schools another reason is they want to remove their children from the violence and drug use, which is running rampant in our government-run school system. A third reason is parents want to remove their children from the government-run school system because of the poor education their children will receive there.

The elected officials of the United States government send their children to private schools, at least the ones who care about their children's education. The ones, who are trying to make a political statement by ruining their children's future, send their children to government-run schools. Maybe we should force all of our elected officials to send their children to the government-run school, and then we could see how fast the government-run school system gets fixed. Politicians don't solve problems they regulate them until it hits their home. Then the problem is solved.

We can see that there are at least two forms of our corruption that matched that of Rome's corruption. When Rome's politicians would do anything to keep power, did they do what our liberal politicians are doing today? The Democrats promote class envy, victimhood, and gift giving of taxpayers' resources, while trying to get everyone on the public dole. This type of politicking can only be subsidized for a short period of time. You do need people working to pay taxes, which pay the bills of the state governments and the federal government. Republicans, on the other hand, aren't much better. They do almost as much. Instead of standing firm in their constituents' beliefs, they give Democrats 80% of what they want.

This might be why the Democrats have had power in Congress for over 40 years and why our country is in the shape it's in.

One other similar corruption that we have in common with the Roman Empire is the consistent budget cutting of our military, when Democrats get in power. Rome at first believed in having a strong military, but as time went on and they developed apathy and a complacent lifestyle, security of their nation did not seem that important. They started cutting military spending, their military suffered from budget cuts and loathing from some of its people. This is what we are seeing today from the Democratic Party; a loathing of our military.

I wonder if this is an attempt to get people to stop joining our military. If you can recreate the loathing of our military personnel as was done during the Vietnam War, you will get a reduction in reenlistment along with new enlistments. Less people joining the military means less money needed to fund your military, but in this process of reducing your military you reduce your readiness.

It took Rome a long time to finally fall. So what started Rome's decline? What were the warning signs that the Romans should have been heeding? One warning sign, should have been their weaken military. Another sign would have been their financial problems. The one sign that was totally ignored was their illegal immigration problem, which probably was the main reason for their fall as a nation.

"Economic factors are cited as a major cause of the Fall of Rome."[5] Some historians say that Rome's decline started back in 106 A. D., when Rome started to have financial problems. Some say that her financial problems started earlier, while others say it started a little later, but they all seem to agree that it started around the second century A.D. When did we start to have money problems?

Why did Rome last for another 370 years? Did Rome's permanent spilt in 395 A.D. give her a reprieve? No, not really. What it did do was weaken the west while strengthening the east. The Western Roman Empire struggled for survival for roughly another century.

I find these two statements rather interesting, because I see this happening in the United States right now. "In 118 A.D. Hadrian agreed to wipe off a bad debt to the treasury, which amounted to the equivalent of £7 million and also reduced many sums, which were outstanding for rent."[6] "However, when the citizens of the empire could not afford to pay at all then simply reducing debts was not a long-term answer."[7] Is this what's going to happen to us under the Barack Obama's administration?

I believe we will see the United States government face the same situation as time goes on. The Roman Empire "got to the stage when tax-payers simply had to pay what was demanded of them, meaning that the State would necessarily have to become strengthened."[8] We are seeing the growth of the United States government, which in turn means the growth of the bureaucracy of government, which means that our tax burden will get worse.

Rome grew their government, which in turn caused "the growth of the bureaucracy and a parallel development of what we today would call the 'police-state.'"[9] "During the pax romana we see a very sad state of affairs emerging, whereby the only means of keeping the empire funded was through legalized extortion".[10] I believe the United States has reached this stage in our history.

How much longer will we last with the money problems we are having? I'm not quite sure, but I believe times were different. Back then, news traveled slower. One nation's financial problems didn't necessary affect another nation, unless they were allies and that ally was dependent on your money to fund their security. Sort of like Israel. They need our financial support for their survival. In today's world, our money problems are having an impact on the world's economy, and every nation knows about our financial difficulties in a matter of minutes.

We were borrowing money from China, which was a bad move, but now the Chinese government has told us that they are not going to buy any more of our debt. They are having doubts that we can pay back the money. Anyway, once you become indebted to another nation, they have power over you, and can bring you to financial collapse by calling in your debt.

Importing of oil has indebted us to Arab countries and has weakened our nation's security among foreign nations. Our lack of will to tap into our own resources because of a small radical group has made us dependent on other nations, which has made us weak and accessible to foreign pressures.

The nation of France has called for us, the United States, to pay a world tax. What I'm seeing from our weak-kneed mealy mouthed politicians is that they will go along with it, which means we probably will start paying this tax. We have Senators in our Congress proposing that we raise our payment to the United Nations, which will help support their attempts to help the poor nations of the world. We can't keep welfare in our own borders. We now have to export it. This must be from the "hate and blame America first" crowd. I don't know about you, but I feel I pay enough taxes and I don't want to pay any more.

So, did this happen during the Roman days? To the extant we have it today, not at first, because Rome conquered its territories when they were a republic. Their problems started when they changed to an empire form of government around the first century A.D. Due to their financial strains in the second century A.D., they went from an offensive posture to a defensive posture. They later split their empire in half.

In 122 A.D., Hadrian had a wall built in England and strengthened other border defenses around the Roman Empire. Rome's financial problems stayed inside her borders, but by building these border defenses, Rome had to find the money from within their borders to defend themselves, which added to their financial problems.

When Rome asked some of their citizens to lower their lifestyle, is when their country started to suffer. People don't like it when they have to suffer for something they can't see any benefit from. I wonder if they saw the need for a strong military once they got sacked in 410A.D. It doesn't show that in history, because Rome got sacked again in 455A.D. I wonder, after they fell from power, if they saw the need to lower their lifestyle and sacrifice a little for the security of their nation. Hindsight is always 20/20. Once Rome did fall from power, their lifestyle was lowered, willingly or not. They had less than what they were accustom, to having.

Even though Rome was having money problems, they still had a powerful army in the region. Only in their 4th and 5th century did Rome's army start to show real signs of weakness. We have the most powerful army on the face of the Earth, but we lack the will to fight. I believe that this was brought on by our political correctness. I think the Romans lost their will to fight.

We today have liberal politicians in the United States trying to destroy our military self-esteem. Liberal politicians will badmouth our military every chance they get and will try to cut funding to our military at every opportunity.

At first Rome's money came from plundering other nations' wealth. Then Hadrian became emperor, and in 122 A.D. he ordered the Roman legions to abandon their offensive posture and go to a defensive posture. I'm sure he thought that this would ease Rome's financial burdens. Rome found out later how wrong he was.

We won World War II by turning the tides on the Germans by getting them into a defensive posture. We are seeing this today on the war on terror. Terrorist groups are trying to get us in a defensive posture with the aid of some liberal politicians in Washington.

Hadrian's decision to go to a defensive posture added to Rome's financial problems. For Rome to keep their military strong and their borders defended, they had to find the men and finances to support their army from within their own borders. This meant raising the taxes on Roman citizens. They also reduced their development of new weaponry. We're seeing that today, with our military. We have reduced the research and development of military weaponry since the 1960s. Rome's readiness to fight was impaired by the army's lack of equipment and the reduced quality of equipment. Our readiness was impaired to fight after having eight years of Bill Clinton as President. He cut military spending by 50% and forced members of our armed forces into early retirement.

What was once an honor to Roman citizens, which was to serve in their armed forces, now became a burden. Respect for the military fell. No one wanted to serve. The Roman citizens found ways to get out of serving in the military. So Rome used barbarian mercenaries to fill their ranks. So what are we going to do, when the respect of our military suffers from the badmouthing from our liberal politicians? Are we going to go back to a draft system? Are we going to fill our ranks with foreigners? Will we have to lower our lifestyle to keep our military strong, as some of the Roman citizens did?

We're being asked to lower our lifestyle for the global warming hoax, but not to keep our military strong. This is interesting. We can't lower our lifestyle for our military to keep us safe, but we are being asked, to lower our lifestyle for a hoax and a scam such as global warming.

Will we lower our lifestyle for this hoax? I believe we will because we are so gullible. We won't lower our lifestyle for the security of our nation, but we will for global warming. I can see people falling for this hook, line, and sinker. So why would a liberal politician, such as Al Gore, call for this, and why would he do this to us? I believe this is done to put more control over us and to get the tax dollars they want us to pay under this false pretense.

I always ask this question to people who come up to me and start talking about global warming: Do you know anyone who would lower their lifestyle to promote a lie? I always get the same answer: No. Then I tell them that I don't see any liberals, especially Al Gore, setting any examples by lowering their lifestyle. I don't see them refusing to use their personal jet aircrafts, or see them refusing to drive a car that gets six miles to a gallon of gasoline, to reduce their greenhouse gas emissions. When I see Al Gore do this, then I will do the same.

The Imminent Fall of the United States

Chapter 15

It is amazing to me that we the people of the United States are allowing our elected representatives, of the United States government, to make the same mistakes that other superpowers have made in the past. It is interesting to me that most historians of our time have kept silent or refuse to comment on these mistakes.

Some liberal politicians are commenting about how we should learn from the past, but their comments on the past are selective, used to promote their agenda. In other words, they are only giving us half the historical event. One way to see if people are quoting half of an historical event is to study the history they are referring to.

Liberal Democrats do this with the Bible as well. They will miss-quote the word of God to advance their political agenda. So, whatever happened to non-biased professionalism? People who would state the facts and let the chips fall where they may. Liberal Democrats don't want facts to get in the way of their agenda, whether it is historical facts or present-day facts. We are seeing this being played out in the global warming legislation.

I am dumbfounded by the lack of interest the people of our country have in our imminent fall from world power. Why do we the people of this nation have such a devil-may-care attitude toward the welfare of our country? Is it because political correctness is more important than the welfare and security of our nation? It is politically correct to allow 20 million illegal immigrants to come into our country and do nothing about it. It is politically correct to give amnesty to them, but don't you dare talk about putting up a fence to keep them out. So it must be politically incorrect to put up a fence to keep them out. If you complain about the lack of security our nation has, to keep foreigners out of our country, you will have your character attacked by liberal political hack groups, or you're insensitive to the plight of others.

We have people in this country who care more about their political power than the security of the United States. If it is political expedient to disregard our security as a nation, they will do so. If they can seize a political opportunity to gain power, even if it means the destruction of the United States, they will do that too. Some will use their political power to pass laws so they may have more power over us, while weakening our nation. Their activity hurts us in the long run, the citizens of the United States. Every superpower in the past has faced some type of corruption and everyone has fallen. Why do you think we will be any different?

The type of corruption we are facing today from our politicians is nothing new. So how did we allow this to happen? To put it simply: we stopped caring. One other possibility is that we plunged ourselves so deep into debt that we have to work two jobs to make ends meet. This means that we have little time to check up on our elected officials and our children, if you have children.

This is why I believe this was planned by the politicians in Washington. They want us to be too busy to check up on them. That way it is easier for them to get their legislation passed. Also by us being so busy, we have a tendency to believe that the politician representing our district is doing a good job. This could be the furthest thing from the truth, but since we are so busy working, we wouldn't know how he/she is doing. How long are we going to do this? Probably until we fall from world power and then it will be too late.

What is funny to me, the first thing some of our elected officials want to do when times get tough is to cut military spending. This is typical for liberal Democrats. Programs that were enacted for their special interest groups are more important than our safety.

These programs were created for two reasons. One: to pay back their supporters. Two: to hold power over a group of people, in our country. This is to ensure that they get re-elected to their office. So we as a whole have our safety compromised for the good of our elected politicians.

Is it too late for us? It depends. If we start looking at the activities of the politicians and if their activities are only for their benefit, then we need to vote them out of office. A person who runs for public office and has the attitude of "I'm first and the country is second," should never be elected to that office. Unfortunately, I believe that the majority of our elected officials have that attitude.

One way to find out if these elected officers are doing our will is to give them a test. One test I think we should give them is: to see if they would be willing to impeach some of the rogue Supreme Court justices and Nancy Pelosi the speaker of the House of Representatives. How many of you are outraged that the Supreme Court feels that terrorists, people who want to kill you and me, as soon as they see us, are entitled to the same rights we have under our Constitution?

Spies and terrorists should never be given the same rights we enjoy under our Constitution. How many of you are tired of the Supreme Court justices quoting foreign law, to judge a case in favor of the political agenda? How many of you are getting tired of the Supreme Court overruling the will of the people? How many of you are getting tired of Nancy Pelosi running the House of Representatives as the queen of the United States, not allowing any up or down votes when it is not on her list of agendas.

What is interesting to me, and hopefully to you, is we had a stimulus package passed under George Bush's presidency, to try to shore up our economy. Where did we get this money? Well, we borrowed it from China. By doing so, we plunged our nation deeper into debt. Now under Barack Obama's presidency we just recently had another stimulus package passed. Has it helped? I haven't seen any economic activity. What I have seen is things have gotten worse. General Motors and Chrysler filed for bankruptcy.

Some say the debt we have shoved onto the next generation is $53 trillion. I for one think it is better to pay off our debt and have a slight slowdown than to push this kind of debt onto our grandchildren and great-grandchildren.

To keep borrowing money that we can't pay back is poor money management on our part. If the Chinese ever call in the debt we have with them, what do you think will happen to us? We will have an economic slowdown that will make the Great Depression look like a cakewalk. So let's just keep on working and not care what our incompetent representatives are doing in Washington.

By the way, everyone who raves about the economy when Bill Clinton was president is blowing smoke at you. The economy under Clinton's presidency was worse than the economy under the presidency of George Bush 43. The worst rate of unemployment under George Bush 41 presidency was 7.5%, in 1992. [1] The unemployment rate when Clinton took office was 6.1%. You can see from that, before Clinton took office we were coming out of our recession. A year later, it was 6.9%; this was probably caused by Bill Clinton's tax increases. [2] During 1994, the unemployment rate fell to 6.1%. In 1995 the unemployment rate fell to 5.6%, I believe this happened because we gave the Republican Party the control of the House of Representatives and the Senate, due to the 1994 elections.

Why do I think this was due to the Republicans' control of the House and the Senate? Well, we gave the Democrats control of both houses in 2006, and gasoline rose to $4 per gallon. Unemployment rose to 8.1% in 2008; it was 4.5% in 2006.

Let's get back to Bill Clinton's economy. In 1996 the unemployment rate was 5.4%. I just don't see this so-called great economy of Bill Clinton's. In 1997, the unemployment rate was 4.9%. Your argument of a great economy might start to take hold here. Now who was responsible for it, the Congress or the President? I believe the Congress was responsible. The years of 1998, 1999 and 2000 did have low unemployment rates. In 1998, the rate was 4.5%; this matches the unemployment of 2006. In 1999, the rate was 4.2% and the rate for 2000 was 4.0%. [3] These numbers might be a little bogus, due to the fact that while Bill Clinton was in office he had the books cooked.

When George Bush 43 took office in 2001, the unemployment rate was 4.7%. Economists said that this was because of the Clinton years; maybe I'm not an economist. This is the way I look at the unemployment rates, as a foundation to our economy. When you're unemployed, you are in a depression. While times are tough and you're working, you are in a recession. Unemployment reached 5.8% in 2002. This was the worst year of unemployment until 2008. So why do we give credit to Bill Clinton and ignore President Bush's achievements? We are lazy or too busy to check for ourselves. So we believe the lies the liberal Democrats tell us along with their lackeys in the news media. Here is also the tax burden under both presidents. [4]

TAXES UNDER CLINTON 1999	**TAXES UNDER BUSH 2008**
Single making 30K - tax $8,400	Single making 30K - tax $4,500
Single making 50K - tax $14,000	Single making 50K - tax $12,500
Single making 75K - tax $23,250	Single making 75K - tax $18,750
Married making 60K - tax $16,800	Married making 60K- tax $9,000
Married making 75K - tax $21,000	Married making 75K - tax $18,750
Married making 125K - tax $38,750	Married making 125K - tax $31,250

I was hoping that Barack Obama wouldn't hurt our country's employment any more than he already has, but it seems that he is dead set on harming the American corporations. How is hurting the American corporations going to hurt employment? I'm not an economist, but I know that if you raise taxes on the American corporations, you are going to hurt their competitiveness, which means more people will buy foreign goods because they are cheaper.

The United States government tax rates on the American corporations are higher than the tax rates of Sweden. Yes, Sweden has a lower tax rate on its corporations than the United States does. Now, how is Barack Obama going to hurt the American corporations any more than they already are? He plans to close the tax deduction (loopholes) on the American corporations. He thinks by punishing them for going overseas, to get some work done will help our economy.

So, what's wrong with leaving the welfare of our country and of our families, in the hands of our elected officials? I, for one, think that their track recorded isn't what it should be. Since the 1960s, we have put $9 trillion into welfare programs. Has it helped? I don't see it, if anything I believe it has made things worse. What has welfare done for the poor? It's done nothing, except for destroying one of the strongest-knit family structures this country ever had. Welfare promotes single parenting, illegitimacy, and abortion. Refer to chapter 4.

The Murdering of the Innocent

When a country murders their young, they destroy their future, "on average, about 3,500 to 3,700 babies are aborted everyday" in our country. [5] I find this to be amazing. Why do we allow 3,500 to 3,700 murders of the innocent a day? How do we know that we have this many murders of the innocent in a day? We know this amount by the records of the abortion mills running throughout our country. How did abortions get so high? Well, we have given women the right to commit murder, under the excuse that it is her body and she has the right to do what she wants with it.

This to a Christian is a bogus argument. We are all part of the body of Christ. Therefore, God doesn't allow us to do anything we want to our bodies. We're not allowed to drink to get drunk, to eat food in excess, this is called gluttony in the Bible. We're not allowed to take illegal drugs to get high. We are not allowed to pierce our bodies or tattoo them. Check out Leviticus in the Old Testament if you are wondering about what Christians should be doing with their bodies.

Do I obey every law of God? No, I don't. That's why they are called sins, and we all sin. Now liberals say, since we can't obey God's laws because of our sin nature, we should just forget about them and do what we want. Well, we see what is happening to our country with that type of thinking, but in reality liberals can't even follow their own beliefs. They only want you to break God's laws when it's convenient to them.

Now back to this statement that a woman has a right to do whatever she wants with her body. To a secularist, this is a good argument, hard to counter, except when you apply it to other aspects of "this is my body and I can do what I want with it." Liberal Democrats will argue against anyone who will say: I have the right to drink alcoholic beverages and eat food, to the excess, which will give me health problems. I don't care if it's gluttony. If I become obese and could possibly have a heart attack or stroke, I have that right under the philosophy of "it's my body and I can do what I want with it." If I want to smoke cigarettes to the point of getting lung cancer, what's it to you? I also have the right to charge for my organs, if I want to sell them for transplant when I'm alive. I also have the right to give my family members permission to sell my organs when I'm dead, as long as I authorize this in my last will and testament.

I personally don't want to open Pandora's Box, but I do get tired of liberal Democrats passing bills for the President of the United States to sign so they will become laws, which allows their double standards to be put upon me. They do this mainly because of their emotional outburst of feeling instead of rationally thinking thing through.

Why would liberal Democrats start arguing against this? Isn't it your body and don't you have a right, to do, what you want with it? Isn't this their argument on abortion? Could it be that all the other statement about "this is my body," doesn't fit their agenda? Could it be about high rates of health care costs? Why do they feel they have the right to tell you how to live? Why do they feel that it is okay to murder the unborn, but not allow someone else to kill themselves slowly? Why do liberals say you should use preventive medicine, to stop us from having health problems?

They will preach to us about how preventive medicine will lower the high costs of health insurance. What I don't see from these people is the same arguments used on women who get pregnant and have abortions. I don't see them arguing to women that they should use preventive methods so they don't become pregnant. This would cause women to have fewer abortions, which I think would help keep our health care costs down. The less you use the health care system, the lower the costs should be. This is economics 101; the supply and demand rule does apply here.

Do liberal politicians and liberal organizations have the right to argue that we should live a healthier lifestyle, to lower our health care costs? Yes, they have that right, and I probably would listen to them if they applied this argument across the board to all unhealthy activities. Our perverted western society lifestyle does add to our health care costs. New medical health care machines, designed to find health problems, add to the health care costs we are seeing today.

The health factors are also somewhat of a bogus argument, because if this person wants to have an unhealthy lifestyle, isn't that his/her right to do so? He/she is the one that will answer to God for their activities. I don't believe we should allow these liberal politicians to be our parents and set policy for us. We pay enough in taxes.

What it really boils down to, is that liberal politicians feel they have the right to set policy on how we should live, in our society, even if a majority of us don't want that type of lifestyle. If someone objects to their way of thinking, to their lack of morals or to their socialistic form of government, you suddenly become politically incorrect or you are intolerant. So why, all of a sudden are liberals allowed to use these stereotypical forms of hatred, against someone, who might have a legitimate concern of what liberal politicians and liberal organizations are doing to our country? Some people will tell you that the biggest threat to our nation is liberalism, and I personally agree.

Why hasn't anyone asked a liberal why they are intolerant to the intolerant? I would think that if you are intolerant, and if someone is intolerant to your intolerance, then that person is also intolerant. I for one do not want to live under the policies of liberal Democrats. I don't want to pay higher taxes to support their nanny form of government or their perverse, decadent lifestyles. I think as a society we should strive to have a moral lifestyle. I believe we should try to obey God's laws and we should hold our politicians to these morals.

Is our current type of behavior, which we are engaged in, which is being pushed by liberal Democrats, good for our nation's survival? No, 48 million abortions have happened since it became legal to murder the innocent. By allowing this type of behavior, we have significantly reduced the size of our next generation. By reducing the size of the next generation, we have created a Social Security problem for the elderly. Refer to chapter 1.

Once again, why is it bad to leave the welfare of our country and our families in the hands of our elected officials? Aren't they thinking about the welfare of our country? No, I don't think they are. I think they will do anything to keep power, and if that means selling our country down the river, they will do that with a smile on their faces. One example of that would be Bill Clinton and China. Another example would be our illegal immigration problem.

Illegal Immigration

Illegal immigrants have an easier time getting access to our social programs than we do, the citizens of the United States, who are paying for these services through our tax dollars. Illegal immigrants are adding to the costs of our health insurance. It is estimated that the cost for our illegal immigration problems, in our country is costing the taxpayers $338.3 billion per year. If you don't believe this amount, then check out these web sites and add up the 14 examples for yourselves.

1. Do you think that "$11 Billion to $22 billion being spent on welfare for illegal aliens, each year," by state governments is not a problem? [6]
2. The amount of "$2.2 Billion a year, which is being spent on food assistance programs, such as food stamps, WIC, and free school lunches, is for illegal aliens".[7] Do you think we the tax payers should be paying for this? I don't.
3. I don't think the taxpayer should allow this: "$2.5 Billion a year is spent on Medicaid for illegal aliens."[8]
4. We spend "$12 Billion a year, on primary and secondary school education for children here illegally and they cannot speak a word of English."[9] I think the money should go to the children of United States citizens
5. This amount of money, "$17 Billion a year is spent for education for the American-born children of illegal aliens,

known as anchor babies."[10] One must ask what is left for our children.

6. I think we should send these illegal aliens to an unpopulated island and let them fend for themselves. "$3 Million a day is spent to incarcerate illegal aliens."[11]
7. If we would send these illegal aliens that have committed crimes in our country, to an island, we would free up 30% of space in all our federal prisons. One other way of putting this is; "30% of all federal prison inmates are illegal aliens."[12]
8. This is interesting, "$90 billion a year is spent on illegal aliens, for Welfare & social services" by the American taxpayers."[13] I think we should demand that this be stopped.
9. By allowing illegal aliens in our country we are now having our wages suppressed to the tune of "$200 Billion a year."[14] The only people that can be blamed for this are our elected officials.
10. "The illegal aliens, in the United States, have a crime rate that's two and a half times that of white non-illegal aliens."[15] In question to this, are their children going to be better citizens or worse?
11. We need to do something other than amnesty to solve this problem. "During the year of 2005 there were 4 million to 10 million illegal aliens that crossed our Southern Border, also, as many as 19,500 illegal aliens from Terrorist Countries."[16] Not to mention the "millions of pounds of drugs: cocaine, meth, heroin and marijuana" that crosses into the U.S. from our Southern border. [17]
12. "The National Policy Institute "estimated that the total cost of mass deportation would be between $206 billion to $230 billion, or an average of "between" $41 billion to $46 billion annually over a five year period."[18]
13. "In 2006, illegal aliens sent home $45 Billion in remittances back to their countries of origin."[19]
14. "Nearly One Million Sex Crimes Committed by illegal immigrants in the United States" and politicians in our country

call for amnesty for these people. [20] I think that this is outrageous.

This should show us that our politicians are putting the rights of illegal immigrants above our rights, the citizens of the United States. How's that for a kick in the teeth? The illegal immigration problem has caused a lot of our hospitals to close their doors, because of laws passed which say, people who don't have insurance cannot be refused medical treatment, especially if they are unable to pay for it. Who doesn't have insurance? Illegal immigrants for sure don't have insurance, and some of our middle class.

Politicians say that there are 47 million people in our country without insurance, and since we have 12 million to 20 million illegal immigrants, we can assume that we really have about 27 million people that need help. I question this number, but we'll let it stand for argument's sake.

The question that needs to be asked, here, is how many of these people choose not to have insurance. I by choice chose not to have insurance for a period of years in my life. It was cheaper for me to pay the doctor bills than to pay for health insurance. Now that I'm married and I'm in my 50s, which means I might have more or more significant health problems, I choose to have insurance. So, I believe we shouldn't force people to have insurance who do not want it. So why do liberal Democrats feel they have the right to force you to have insurance? I don't know, probably something to do with the good of the all, which means the ones who can't pay for it will have it paid for them, by the working class of the United States, the people who pay taxes, which means another fiasco in the making.

I don't mind helping out our poor, which means these people that need health insurance, should be put on the Medicaid health care program. I for one surely don't want to pay higher taxes for people who don't belong in our country. Illegal immigrants surely don't have a right to our social programs. For those who feel they do, then they can pull out their wallets and pay for it. I surely haven't seen any liberal Democrats or Republicans do that, which leads to the old saying, "liberals are generous with your money but stingy with theirs." Maybe it should say politicians are generous with our money but stingy with theirs.

Dictatorship of the Two Parties

What does it take to be a politician in the United States? Well, it means you have to be a habitual liar. As soon as politicians open their mouths, they are lying to you. It doesn't matter if you are conservative or liberal. The people you are voting for are lying to you, with a straight face. We know that they are lying to us, but since we live in a two-party dictatorship, there's not much we can do about it. I for one am getting tired of the two-party dictatorship that is forming into a one-party dictatorship. The conservatives are not running the Republican Party anymore. They have allowed liberals to come into their party and have allowed them to destroy the basic foundation of the Republican Party. John McCain is one example of that.

A two-party dictatorship is better than a one-party dictatorship, but if you can't tell the parties apart, if both parties have the same ideals. Then isn't it really a one-party system? If we the people start to vote for third-party candidates, would it help? Yes, for now, but remember the old saying, "Power corrupts and absolute power corrupts absolutely." Term limits is one answer to this problem and politicians have always fought against it. If we put a two-term limit on our elected officials, then they won't be able to create a power base for themselves and their power would be greatly reduced. They actually might start caring about the welfare of our country.

What's the Answer to Stop Our Imminent Fall from World Power?

So what are the answers to stop our imminent fall from world power? I would think we need less government intrusion into our everyday lives. Less government regulations and smaller government would mean fewer taxes. Hopefully by paying less money in taxes, we would have more disposable income, more money in our savings, less government wasteful spending, an economy, which would have less than a 4.0% unemployed rate. This would also give parents more time with their children and less time at work. Hopefully this will start putting our families back together again.

Welfare in its current form needs to be stopped, and a system that puts the family back together again might help our situation.

What answers do our politicians have to stop our fall? The same old answers they always have. What are their answers? They want to add another layer of government to our already big, bloated, inefficient, slow-moving federal government. This is what got us into the troubles we are facing today. A big bloated, inefficient, slow-moving federal government is not the answer. I know liberals will say that the United States became great because of big government. I don't believe it, do you?

The answer is for government to get out of the way and let our country have the free markets it had back in the 1950s. We the people better realize that the larger we allow our government to get, the larger our tax burden will become. Governments get their money through taxation. The more programs they enact, the more money they will need. Our current federal budget is $5.3 trillion, three trillion too much.

If historians did comment on our mistakes, in a non-biased way, would we as a nation listen to them and change our course of destruction? Considering, other nations in the past didn't heed the warnings given to them by their learned society, I don't think we would either. This might be why the non-biased professionals are silent. So let's just face it, our fall is imminent. Now should we quicken our fall and vote liberal, or should we think about the next generation and try to slow it down? If we vote for the liberals, then we have quickened our fall from world power.

Liberals Talk a Good Story Line

Liberals talk a good story line, they are very charismatic people and very likeable. These are three traits they have to have to get people like us, to cut our own throats and enjoy doing it. Bill Clinton and Barack Obama are good examples of charismatic people. John McCain is an example of one who is not; maybe he spent too many years in Vietnam.

Liberals always talk negatively about our current situation. Usually, negative talking people who continually blame and complain about other people, or about a situation are not the people we should be turning to, to fix the problems, we are facing today in our country. Their complaining doesn't solve problems, it usually adds to them.

Barack Obama is a charismatic person with the ability to read a teleprompter. With the aid of his teleprompter, he says nothing with such eloquence that people who have listened to him have voted for him, without understanding what he stands for.

One thing he wants to do is to repeal George Bush's tax cuts and go back to what Bill Clinton did for us back in the 1990s. Barack Obama talked about change, but told us very little about the change, he wanted to bestow upon us, but now we see it and I was right. He has enlarged the federal government, has increased our deficit spending, and has the federal government start nationalizing banks and industry. All of this is done to take more of our freedoms away. Is this the correct form of change?

When liberal Democrats mess things up, they have the ability to blame someone else for their mistakes. They get us to believe that they didn't have anything to do with the fiasco they have created. You see, liberal Democrats don't want to be held accountable for their mess-ups. They want you to judge them, on their feeling and how they care about the situation, but they don't want to be judged by the lack of results from their worthless government programs.

Here are some of the fiascos they have caused: the mortgage fiasco, the welfare fiasco, the Medicare fiasco and the Medicaid fiasco, and now they want to cause the health care fiasco. Ted Kennedy is the father of the HMO insurance programs. This was created to help the poor. Has it? He's the one who got the legislation passed back in 1972. How many people know that or remember that? So with that little bit of knowledge, are we going to allow them to create a health care fiasco? Yes, probably so. When they blame someone else for this potential fiasco, will we believe them? Yes, we probably will.

You can look at any nation in the past and you will see strong opposition to the changes put forth, by people, who cared about the welfare of their country. Status quo is always easier to live with. People will fight to stop change, even if the changes will save their nation. One of the changes, we need to make is to stop taking care of people who don't want to take care of themselves. I will give anyone a hand up. I don't want to give someone a hand out. What's the difference? The difference is that a hand up is given to someone who has fallen on hard times. A hand out is given to those who don't want to take care of themselves.

It is hard to stand on our own two feet today, especially with the huge tax burden we have. That being said, most of us have always strived to take care of ourselves. This has always been one's goal in life. When we were children, we used to fight with our parents to become independent. Now it seems we did that only to take the hand of big nanny government to lead us through adult life.

Changes that our nation should be implementing and following are being ignored, and changes that we should not have implemented are destroying our country. This is why I laugh at people who say change is good. The right change is good; change for change sake is bad. Liberals are master of change, mostly the wrong type of change. Liberals support changes that increase the size of our government, which in turn means higher taxes, which in turn means longer hours at work or maybe a second job, to support this big, bloated, inefficient, slow-moving federal government they are proposing.

Do we really want this type of life, where we allow government to take care of us? Do we want to look like little children to the rest of the world? Do we want the rest of the world to think we have to have our hands held and have all our decisions made for us? We might not, but that's how it's starting to come across, to the rest of the world. We look like weak little children that can't blow our own noses without help from our federal government.

Corrupt Politicians

The people who got our nation into the problems we are facing will not be the people who will get us out of these problems, we are facing. The mindset of these people who got us into these problems will not change. Therefore, we will need to change out these people in power. We will need people who have a different way of thinking. We also need to make sure that when the United States government enacts bad legislation, that that legislation is changed immediately. What would I call bad legislation? I would put welfare, Medicare, the prescription drug benefits and Medicaid under the umbrella of bad legislation.

Why would anyone want a big, bloated, inefficient, slow-moving federal government? Politicians want this type of government so they can accrue power and control over us. When you spend more time working, the less time you have to watch them. Then the more likely, they are, to get legislation passed that you are not aware of.

For instance, the John McCain amnesty bill that almost passed into law. President Bush was going to sign this bill into law. It just didn't make it through the Senate due to our opposition. I also remember that John McCain said that they should pass this bill with very little debate, so that politics wouldn't impede the process. What he really meant, was to get the bill passed before the people of the United States understood what was in the bill. He wanted this bill passed under the cover of darkness. How's that for putting the rights of lawbreakers over the rights of law-abiding citizens? If we allow this big, bloated, inefficient, slow-moving government, which liberals love, to increase in size, it will continue to increase its hold on us. We need to remember that any government big enough to give us anything our heart desires, can and will, take it away from us any time it wants to.

As I stated previously in many of these chapters, corruption is always the cause of a nation's fall. Corruption comes in many different forms. The form of our corruption is politicians who want to keep power at any cost. This eventually will bring on the destruction of our country. This type of corruption is evident in many ways. One of these forms of corruption that comes to my mind, is their constant talk of closing our borders, to illegal immigrants, but doing very little to do so. Most of our politicians favor amnesty for illegal immigrants. The corruption of our politicians is also brought to light by the gift giving to certain groups of people. This is done to buy votes. Some of our politicians close their eyes to lawbreakers, to secure the votes of these people for future elections.

Sounds a little bit like Rome in her latter days. In 455 A.D., a Roman Senator named Petronius Maximums became the next emperor of Rome when Valentinian was assassinated by a follower of Aetius. He then "forced Eudoxia to marry him by threatening her with death, thinking that his position would be more secure."[21]

Our Politicians' Big Mistake

Why do I think that our politicians are making a big mistake about illegal immigrants? Rome's politicians didn't stop illegal immigrants from coming into their country. This gave them a lot of problems. They even had trouble with legal immigrants. Now the Goths (Visigoths) did ask for permission to come into Rome's territory, because they grew tired of fighting with the Huns. I guess the Roman Emperor Valens thought that since Rome defeated the Goths so badly in 367 A.D., to where, "the Goths had to beg for mercy," that they learned their lesson not to mess with the Roman Empire.[22] This was a big mistake on the emperor's part, but hindsight is always 20/20. The Visigoths bided their time and grew powerful. It's a shame that the Roman emperors didn't stay vigilant to the threat of the Visigoths, because the Visigoths did sack Rome in 410 AD.

The Vandals did not ask for permission to cross the Rhine and came into the Western Roman Empire territory, "one cold and frozen night in December" 406 A.D.[23] "They surprised the Romans and breached the Frontier at Mainz."[24] They were met by the Franks and were almost defeated until the Alans came to their aid. The Vandals are one example of people that came into a neighboring country without that country's permission. The Vandals laid waste to the Gallic Empire and they finally settled in Spain in 409 A.D. The devastation that the Vandals caused to the Gallic Empire has given us the word *vandalized.* The Romans in around 418 A.D. employed the Visigoths to evict the Siling Vandals along with the Alans out of Southern Spain. The Visigoths "finally succeed in ruining" the Vandals, but the Romans feared that the Visigoths were "becoming too powerful" and gave them an offer "to settle in southeast Gaul in" 418 A.D. [25]

Around 428 A.D., the Vandals traveled from Spain to northern Africa at the request of a Roman governor. When the Roman governor found out that he didn't need their help and told them to go back to Spain, they had different ideas. The Vandals start to vandalize northern Africa, and the attempts by the Western Roman Empire to stop them didn't have much success. The Western Roman Empire was weakened militarily by the corruption of their politicians and by their financial problems. I'm sure that the Roman's lifestyle also contributed to the situation. So what did the Romans do? They did the only thing they could do: they decided on diplomacy, appeasement really. Is this what we are doing with the illegal immigrants in our country, appeasing them with amnesty because our corrupt politicians in Washington feel there is nothing else they can do? Have our financial problems caused us to use appeasement instead of force on these illegal immigrants?

The Vandals were allowed to set up a federation kingdom to Rome, but soon after that, all attempts to appease the Vandals failed. In 455 A.D. the Vandals sacked Rome. The Western Roman Empire finally fell in 476 A.D.

Terrorism

Chapter 16

Will terrorism be the downfall of the United States, or will we adjust? I hope for the sake of the people of the United States and the rest of the world, that we realize this is a war that will not end in one generation. This war will take several generations of fighting, before it will end. Why do I say this? Because these people who blow themselves up, feel they have nothing to live for. The terrorists, who do have something to live for, are telling the terrorists who have nothing to live for, to go into a crowded populated area and blow, themselves up. If we want to have any hope of changing the minds of these people, we have to give them something to live for.

Liberal politicians said we should have defeated terrorism by now. It shouldn't take seven or eight years to do so. As usual with liberal politicians, they're wrong. We haven't even begun to fight this war on terrorism. It will take a minimum of 20 years to get the upper hand, and maybe another 20 to actually win the war on terrorism. I hope you don't believe them when they just pull something out of the air like that. These kinds of irrational statements that liberal politicians make are the same as the laws they pass with their emotional outbursts.

Terrorists will regroup and launch attacks again when our guard is down. Why is this? We haven't changed their way of thinking. Another way of saying this is we haven't given them anything to live for. We might not be able to give them something to live for, but we could show them, who their real oppressors are. These oppressors are their own governments they live under.

I don't think it will change their point of view, but it is worth a try. I don't believe we can get them to realize that their governments are oppressing them. Once someone has a belief in their mind, it doesn't matter what facts or evidence you show them, to the contrary. They won't believe you. I've seen this with poor people who think the rich are getting tax breaks. It doesn't matter what facts or evidence you show them, they still believe the rich are getting tax breaks.

How do I know that terrorists will regroup and attack again? Israel is a country to look at, when you think about a nation that has been fighting terrorism. The Jews and the Palestinians have been fighting for thousands of years.

Now, this current type of warfare Israel is engaged in is terrorism, which has been going on for over 50 years. Is there any end in sight for Israel? No, there isn't. The only way for the Jewish people to have peace is for Israel to cease to exist. So that being said, any concessions given to the Palestinians are a waste of time and effort. All of Israel's Middle Eastern enemies have said something along these lines: Israel doesn't have a right to exist. So why are we constantly telling Israel to give concessions to these people?

Do you think that the Israelites are wining this war on terrorism? I don't. I think it is a stalemate. The liberals of the world are tying the hands of the Israelites behind their backs, and in return giving terrorists a free rein to attack Israel at will. You can't win a war with your hands tied behind your back. Just ask anyone who has fought in the Vietnam War.

Do you think, as I think that Israel is in a stalemate situation with this war on terrorism? Do you think, as I do that right now, Israel is faced with a war on terrorism that will be a never-ending battle? I believe for Israel to have a chance, the world's view has to change toward Israel. We have to untie their hands and let them fight the terrorists.

It is funny how people will act like electricity; they will follow the path of least resistance. In the case of Israel, they will tell Israel to give concessions to terrorists. They know that Israel cannot stand alone, so they threaten them with cutting off financial and military aid. The United States threatens them, with our military alliance. If they don't do what we want, then they won't get financial aid or be able to buy any military hardware from us.

So why do I think, we could win our war on terrorism in 40 years? I believe that once the people of the United States realize that we have to go all out, we will do whatever it takes for our nation to have peace. As of right now, we can't be threatened financially or militarily. That might change, now that we have the appeasers running our federal government.

One way for us to win this war on terrorism is to find them something to live for. If we can't find that something, then we will have to face reality and realize that this war is not winnable in the way we are currently fighting. Anyone who has studied history will tell you that once someone is in a situation where death is better than life, you have the condition that starts rebellions.

In China during the Han Dynasty, the Yellow Turban Rebellion got started because people were starving to death. Not because there wasn't any food, but because the government was taking all the food in taxes. The Russian Revolution got started by women not having any food to feed their babies.

Can we win this war by being able to think like these terrorists? If we started to think like these terrorists, then we should realize that they will wait until we let our guards down and then they will attack us again. They will wait until we have a false sense of security by saying the war is over, then they will attack us. They will carry out attacks of revenge (terrorism) after we retaliate for their original attacks on us. These people have long memories and will keep a grudge that will be passed down from generation to generation. This type of warfare will be known as their legacy.

You have seen a little example of a grudge that has been held onto for two centuries. This grudge was between the Serbians and the Albanians. The Serbians wanted revenge for atrocities, which were done to them under the Ottoman Empire. They launched attacks against the Islamic Albanians.

If a people can wait for two centuries for revenge, do you actually believe that these people can be reasoned with? I doubt that these types of people, with this type of mentality, can be reasoned with.

Our involvement in the region under the Clinton administration did not change their way of thinking. I believe that this is part of human nature, so why do people react to this human nature while others don't? I am not a psychologist, but I believe one of the reasons some people seek out revenge is because they have nothing to live for. In some cases, they are only waiting until they have the upper hand, and let's not forget that people have to avenge the death of a loved one.

Terrorists will regroup if you defeat them once. They will wait and will bide their time, then they will attack when they think you have dropped your guard. The Obama Administration has forced us to drop our guard. So I wouldn't be surprised to see another major attack on our soil by terrorists. The Bush Administration will be blamed for it. That's a must for liberals. They must blame someone else for their failures.

These terrorists have nothing but their memories, which causes them to launch attacks of revenge. To them, this is something to live for. They feel that they have been oppressed by Israel and the United States. They also feel that their land has been stolen from them by Israel. So to them, their oppressors are the United States and Israel. Therefore, we must be dealt with, and terrorism is their only means of getting our attention. To us, it's the wrong kind of attention getting, but to them it will work.

These terrorists will remember our counter-attacks on their terrorist organizations. We must realize that this is going to be a long and bloody war, which will have high casualties on the civilian side, because that is where the war will be taken. Terrorists will not attack military bases, they're not equipped for that. Plus, they would suffer heavy casualties. Now I'm not trying to spread doom and gloom, but please realize that Muslim extremists do not forgive or forget. It is not in their nature, they don't think the same way we do. They only understand force and the use of it.

The question now, is why were we attacked and why did Osama Bin Laden, declare war on the United States. Was it because he saw how soft Bill Clinton was on terrorism, or was it because the United

States was in the Persian Gulf supporting Israel? Or could it have been that the United States has military bases in his home country, so he wanted us to leave the region? I for one don't mind leaving his country, letting them fend for themselves. Hopefully these terrorists will then see that we are not oppressing them, but that their own governments are their oppressors.

Could we declare the Monroe Doctrine and still support Israel? I believe we could. The Monroe Doctrine was created to tell England and other Europeans countries to get out of our region of the world. We can use this, to leave the Arab countries upon their request, but if Israel asks for our help, then we should support them. So let's implement the Monroe Doctrine and leave the Arab nations and let them fend for themselves, while we support our ally Israel. If they feel that Israel doesn't have the right to exist, that's fine, but we do feel that they have that right, and we will support them in their efforts to exist.

Has the Monroe Doctrine ever been effective? No, not really. The Monroe Doctrine was introduced in 1823, soon after the war of 1812. The war of 1812 got started, by us declaring war on England for taking our citizens off our ships. The British forced our citizens to fight for Britain, in a war against the French. The British also came over into our country to try to stir up trouble between us and the Indian nations. So no, the Monroe Doctrine was a failure back then, as all U.N. resolutions are today.

Do terrorist's attacks happen to nations that get complacent? Did the terrorists attack us for revenge over our attack on the country of Sudan, which was ordered by Bill Clinton? Were we attacked in 2001 because of Bill Clinton's actions? If so, we got attacked because Bill Clinton wanted to get his name out of the newspapers and off the TV news media reports. Bill Clinton worried more about what this bad publicity would do to his legacy, than for the good of our country. I don't think the government of Sudan was exactly happy with us, when we launched a sneak attack on them in 1999.

Why did this Islamic terrorist leader, Osama Bin Laden, have his followers attack us? Did he see that the eight years of the Clinton's presidency and the lack of military spending weakened us to a point, where a successful attack could be made? Our military under the

Clinton Administration was at 40% of what it was during the Gulf War. If our military spending wasn't cut so radically, do you think that this attack might not have happened?

Military spending is not just buying hardware, it is also intelligence gathering, and you need good people to do this. Do we have people in place who can handle this type of work, or do we have people that are incompetent? I was talking to a member of a think tank back in the late 1990s, and I asked her if she ever ran any scenarios on countries forming alliances with terrorists. Her reply was no, it was a waste of time, it would never happen. So not being deterred, I asked her about just terrorist organizations launching sneak attacks on us, and again she replied by saying it would never happen. Yes, she was a liberal, and yes, she was wrong, and we suffered the consequences of her refusal to examine any of these types of scenarios. Was she just following orders that her supervisor gave her? That's possible.

We need people to be more proactive instead of reactive. We need a Congress that is not looking to close or do away with our CIA, but to enhance it. We need to tell Maxine Waters, to stop trying to find ways of undermining our intelligence-gathering community, but to find ways to improve it. We need to have an intelligence-gathering community that can find out what is happening in this world. We now have to fight a war, which has come to our doorstep, and we better get serious about it.

We can thank the liberal Democrats for having the stupidity and reluctance to spend the money needed to keep our nation safe from domestic and foreign aggression. We have to tell politicians to stop playing politics with our nation's security and start taking the threats to our security seriously.

I wonder if these people playing politics have any feelings. Are they hurting for their lack of insight on world affairs? I wonder if they realize that the budget cuts they enacted on our military weren't justified and prudent. The Democrats were arguing about $34 billion in tax cuts a week before the terrorist attack. They didn't have enough of our money to spend, so they went with one of the oldest ploys they had in their arsenal. They started a fear tactic that our Social Security surplus will be depleted if we allowed this tax cut to go through. I thought that the Social Security was funded by a separate tax? After the attack on September 11, 2001, it was fine to spend extra money to fight terrorism.

Who's to Blame for These Terrorist Attacks?

Who's to blame for the terrorist attacks that were made on the United States? I believe it is Bill Clinton and the liberal Democrats. One of the first things Bill Clinton did in his first year in office was to cut our military budget by $180 billion. His excuse was Russia was no longer a threat, but his real reason was, he wanted more money for social programs.

Have you noticed that when anyone ever expressed a concern about the lack of money being spent on our military, the liberal Democrats would say that our military could handle any threat the world could throw at us? They were wrong, and I see the biased liberal news media didn't call them on it. The only thing that the liberal TV news media shows are special reports, which show how much money our military, is wasting.

This is funny to me. Our military is one of the most efficient government departments, and if they think the military is wasting money, you then have to ask how much are the inefficient government departments wasting? I would think these departments, which are half as efficient, such as welfare, are wasting double the amount of money our military does.

As I have said before, military spending is not just buying hardware, it is also intelligence gathering, and we need to put people in the field. Our satellites and spy planes have given us a false sense of security. We need to adjust this before it's too late

Liberals Don't like Terrorist Profiling

It seems that liberal Democrats and liberal organizations don't like criminal profiling, they call it racial profiling. Why would they call it that? Is it so they can undermine the attempt to stop terrorism, or could it be their attempt, to look, as if they are standing up for the rights of individuals accused of terrorism? I believe it's to undermine the war on terrorism. So let's look at who has done terrorist acts over the last 40-some years, and see if we have any evidence to prove that one race, of people, have done these barbarian attacks.

In 1968, Robert Kennedy "was assassinated by Sirhan Sirhan a Jordanian Arab Palestinian."[1] In 1972 at the Munich Olympics, Jewish athletes were kidnapped. "Within 24 hours, 11 Israelis, five terrorists, and a German policeman were dead."[2] These deaths were caused by Muslim extremists. In 1979, the United States embassy in Iran was attacked and "Fundamentalist Islamic students took 52 Americans hostage."[3] Why did they do this? Muslim extremists wanted to force the United States to do something in exchange for the hostages.

During the 1980s, "an American-Israeli from Alexandria Virginia, was killed in a PLO attack on Jewish worshippers walking home from a synagogue."[4] A number of Americans were also kidnapped in Lebanon by Muslim extremists, in the attempt to set up negotiations with the United States, and to force them to come to an agreement with them for the exchange of the hostages.

In 1983, "A truck loaded with a bomb crashed into the lobby of the U.S. Marines' headquarters in Beirut."[5] Muslim extremists blew up the U.S. Marines' barracks, in an attempt to force the United States out of Lebanon. In 1985, "the Palestine Liberation Front (PLF), hijacked the Italian cruise ship *Achille Lauro* and demanded the release of Palestinian prisoners held in Israel."[6] A 70-year-old American passenger was murdered and thrown overboard. In 1985, a hijacking of a TWA aircraft was linked to Hezbollah. "TWA flight 847 is hijacked over the Mediterranean."[7] "U.S. Navy diver Robert Dean Stethem is killed and 39 passengers are held hostage, when the demands were not met."[8] In 1988, "a bomb destroys Pan Am 103 over Lockerbie, Scotland."[9] "All 259 people aboard the Boeing 747 are killed including 189 Americans, as are 11 people on the ground."[10] This probably was done for revenge for the attack on Libya, by the United States. Who did this? It was done by Muslim extremists.

In 1993, the World Trade Center was bombed by Muslim extremists, "killing 6 and injuring at least 1,040 others."[11] In 1998, Muslim extremists bombed the U.S. embassies in Kenya and Tanzania, "truck bombs exploded almost simultaneously near 2

U.S. embassies, killing 224 (213 in Kenya and 11 in Tanzania) and injuring about 4,500."[12]

Why? Because Osama Bin Laden declared war on the United States. In 2000, Muslim male extremists fighting a war that Osama Bin Laden had declared on the United States attacked the *U.S.S. Cole*, which was "heavily damaged when a small boat loaded with explosives blew up alongside it."[13] You know what happened on 9/11/2001 in New York City and in Washington, D.C., Muslim extremists hijacked four airliners and two of them were flown into the WTC, one into the Pentagon buildings. In this attack of terrorism, more than 2,800 people were murdered.

In 2001, the United States attacked Afghanistan in retaliation for the attack on 9/11/2001. The United States' attack was against Muslim extremists, who were fighting Osama Bin Laden's war against the United States. In 2002, reporter Daniel Pearl was kidnapped and murdered, by Muslim male extremists who were trying to get the United States into negotiations for his release, but our government said we don't negotiate with terrorists.

Liberals have said that there's no pattern anywhere that would justify profiling of Muslims. Well, I guess we'll just have to look for 80-year-old women who look suspicious.

What is Terrorism and How Do We Win the War on Terrorism?

The definition of terrorism, in ***Webster's Dictionary,*** is: "The use of violence and threats, to intimidate or coerce for political purposes."[14] I believe the definition of terrorism needs to be revised. To me, terrorism is, for a lack of a better word, a refinement from guerrilla warfare. So what is the definition of guerrilla warfare? Well, according to Webster's, the definition is: "The use of surprise raids, sabotage etc., by small, mobile groups of irregular forces operating in enemy territory."[15] Although ***Webster's Dictionary*** doesn't say it, guerrilla fighters also use terrorist attacks on collaborators.

Terrorists use the same tactic as guerrilla fighters, except they use them mainly on civilian targets and civilians; military bases can protect themselves from these types of attacks. Terrorist attacks are also done to create chaos and fear in the civilian population, along with an attempt to get the civilian population involved in the political situation. Terrorists believe that if you hurt the civilian population enough, they will force their government, in our case the federal government of the United States, to negotiate with them. They believe that if they can inflict enough terror into a society, the people of that society will tell their government to give them what they want.

Guerrilla warfare is a very tough war to fight. If you don't have the all-out desire to win or to use the same tactics as the guerrilla fighters, you will lose. Why is this? Guerrilla fighters don't fight a war in a conventional way. There are no front lines (enemy lines). All you have to do is look at the Vietnam War to know this.

The United States didn't do well against guerrilla warfare in Vietnam. The politicians in our country refused to allow our armed forces to use the same tactics as the guerrilla fighters. Most so-called civilized countries won't use these tactics.

We went into Vietnam with the intention of performing a police action. Keep South Vietnam from falling to North Vietnam's aggression. We failed. Why is that? In the end result, North Vietnam conquered South Vietnam.

So how are we going to win the war on terrorism, which is a refinement from guerrilla warfare? Hopefully we will fight this war differently than the Vietnam War. Hopefully we will have the desire to go all-out to win, and will use some of the tactics our enemy is using. I know what you are thinking; you must think I'm smoking something. The United States is too caught up in political correctness, to go on an all-out war on terrorism. We don't want to hurt someone's feelings.

Although I don't have the stomach for it, I'm sure we can find some people who do. So what tactics should we use? We could use one of the tactics that was used in the Philippines at the turn of the 20th century. The tactic used is quite barbaric, but effective.

A pit was dug, and 10 or so pigs were butchered and put into the pit. Terrorists convicted of crimes against humanity were condemned to death by firing squad. The bullets were dipped in pigs' blood and used to shoot the condemned. After they were shot, they were ground up and thrown in the pit with the butchered pigs and covered up. One of the terrorists was spared, and told to tell his friends that this will happen to any terrorist convicted of any crime against humanity.

I think this would work quite well. How about you? I also think pigs should be used in our airports and at any screening area that could have the potential for a terrorist attack. Why would using pigs in this manner be so effective? Muslim beliefs tell them that pigs will desecrate them and will keep them from going to heaven. So they might not want to do any terrorist attacks that would get them killed if a pig has defiled them.

How do we protect Our Citizens When Terrorists Have Gotten Past Our Security?

In the case of terrorists getting on one of our airplanes again, how could we protect our citizens from going through another 9/11? We could give pilots firearms, but I think they should be used as a last resort. We could retrofit all our airplanes with tanks of harmless sleep gas, which could be controlled by the pilots, who turn on a switch, if a hijacking is in progress. If the terrorist has a shoe bomb on the plane and he's about to light the fuse, then the sleep gas would be a bad idea. Therefore, accurate information has to come from the flight attendants. If the sleep gas doesn't work because they have gas masks on, then the last resort would have to be used, which means the pilots would have to use their firearms.

So why should the pilots use their firearms as a last resort? Well, if the sleep gas was tried first and worked, then the plane would be intact and hopefully no one would be hurt. We then could get our revenge on the terrorists by putting them on trial, in a military court of law for terrorism. If they used firearms, an innocent person might get shot instead of a terrorist. That is why I would only want to see firearms used as a last resort.

Religion

Chapter 17

So why is there a religion chapter in this book that shows how liberal utopianism is destroying the United States? To warn the people of the United States, and the world, in the hopes that they might become right with God, because I believe you have to become right with God, before we can have any chance of fixing what's wrong with our nation, the world, and our families. It also shows the liberal Democrats' agenda, which has caused our government to become more atheistic by the day. There is an attack on the Christian's way of life, in our country that seems to be lead by liberal organizations with the aid of liberal Democrats.

How can I say such things? After all, liberal Democrats are the ones who care so much for us. They are the parents we never had and should never have. These liberal Democrats want to replace God with the government and have us accountable to them, but they want to be accountable to no one.

I don't know about you, but I'm an adult and I don't need liberal Democrats or liberal organizations to decide what is good or what is bad for me. How much money I should keep from my earnings, and how I should behave, with their political correctness book of slavery as my guide. I am a Christian. Therefore I put my hope and trust in God, my salvation in Jesus Christ, and the Holy Spirit to protect me from evil, to give me wisdom when needed.

As a Christian, I believe in a live and let live policy. If someone wants to discuss my faith and what I believe in, then I'm willing to discuss that with them. I don't believe in forcing my beliefs on someone else. Now that being said, I find it interesting that liberal organizations, with the aid of liberal Democrats, have to attack my religion every chance they get. I don't understand how they can condone every other religion out there but mine.

Soon our country will rival China in the 1960s to the 1970s, if not surpassing China, and become the most atheistic country on the face of the earth. In China, in the 1960s and 1970s, a Bible was worth as much as a bike, which shows how well the atheists did in eradicating Christianity from the land of China. I find this to be interesting, even though the majority of the people living in the United State, as well as the people living in China, are not atheists. This doesn't seem to matter to atheists. You must adopt their doctrine of beliefs.

What happened to the freedom to practice your religion without persecution? We need to stop being complacent and realize what the liberal organizations' and liberal Democrats' agenda will do to our country if not stopped. We need to speak out and stop this wave of anti-Christianity from destroying our way of life and our country.

Who was it that said? For evil to prosper, good men must do nothing. Right now, the evils of liberalism are prospering. How many times have you heard liberals blasting Christians for not worshiping their political correctness agenda? How many times have you heard downright lies about Christians preaching hatred for their follow man? I believe the preaching of hatred comes mostly from the liberals' ideology and from religions that have a radical fanatical segment to them.

Do liberals embrace these forms of religions? I'm not sure that all liberals do, but most of these religions that have a radical fanatical segment to them, have a form of dictatorship to them. The people that worship their god under the banner of these religions don't have a say in their everyday lives.

You don't believe that liberal Democrats want a dictatorship in our country? Then you need to read chapters 18 and 19. Can you say that liberal Democrats elected into public office are doing the will, of the majority of the people of the United States, or are they doing the will of their special interest groups?

I believe they are doing the will of their special interest groups. The evidence is in the laws they pass, or bills they put forth in an attempt to be passed into laws. Now, should these special interest groups have representation in our government? Absolutely; we live in a country that is supposedly a republic, which means everyone is to have representation.

So what is the problem? Just because you have representation doesn't mean that you have the right to force your beliefs on someone else, or your lifestyle, and expect other people to pay for it. If the majority of the people don't want that law passed by Congress, and it is not unconstitutional, then the minority just has to live with it.

Although people in the United States, says they are a God-fearing nation, the liberal Democratic Party of the United States has managed to stop school prayer. They have managed to have the word God removed from government buildings. Judges have threatened our children with jail time if they mention Jesus as their lord and savior or thank Him for helping them graduate from school.

I thought we didn't have religious persecution in the United States. So why did "a judge decreed that any student uttering the word 'Jesus,' in prayer would be arrested and placed in jail for six months."[1] "The judge also said that anyone who violated his order would wish he or she had died as a child."[2] I thought that we had the right to practice any religion we wanted, which represented the God we believe in and no one had the right to say otherwise?

I believe this judge violated the rights set forth by the First Amendment, which is freedom of speech and freedom of religion. I don't believe that saying thank you to Jesus would cause a riot or cause a stampede for the doors. Our forefathers left their countries of origin to have the right to practice their religious beliefs without persecution, and that is why the First Amendment was set up, to keep this from happening in the United States.

In our country, we can thank the liberal organizations and the liberal Democrats for the endless attacks on the Christian religion. There are many examples of the news media attacking Christian organizations, but the one I will always remember is the attack on Focus on the Family. This is when a gay man was murdered in Wyoming. The liberal news media tried to say that Focus on the Family was preaching violence and hatred against the gay and lesbian communities.

This was a pure fabrication. When James Dobson got on the air after hearing the allegation, he asked his listeners to call the news station and complain about their lack of moral character. Later, the news media asked him to call off his dogs.

When I listened to Focus on the Family, I surely didn't hear any kind of sexual or racial hatred. All I heard was love and compassion for people who chose to remove themselves from God and the hope that one day they will return to God's love and mercy. For a full overview of what happened during those days, you can retrieve a copy of Dr. Dobson's Monthly Letters, titled "It's Not About Hate, It's About Hope," dated November 1998. [3]

I believe there are many reasons why the liberal newspapers and TV news media, are losing their readers and viewers. The Internet is only one aspect of it. People being too busy can be another, but I believe the main reason most people have stopped reading these newspapers and watching the liberal TV news media is because of their biased coverage. The incident with Focus on the Family is only one example.

I believe that the liberal TV news media makes excuses for liberals or doesn't report their activity at all, but condemns conservatives for the same activity. Most people who have a brain can see through this type of biased behavior and find it distasteful.

So why do some liberal politicians and liberal organizations go after the Christian faith and leave other religious faiths alone? I have no idea. Why do some of these liberal politicians cringe when someone proclaims that Jesus Christ is their lord and savior that He died on the cross for our salvation? I don't know. Why do they get so upset when someone says that no one will come to the Father except through Christ Jesus?

I wonder if liberal politicians feel that they can make it on their own, through their good works. I wonder if they hate the idea that they can't get to heaven on their own. They also might hate the fact that they have to answer to someone for their actions.

Liberals, will tell you that there are a lot of religions out there, which will create a lot of good people and that it is not fair to say that their religion, will not get them to heaven. I'm sure there are a lot of religions out there that make people good, which gives them a kind heart and a caring for others. The pastors, the preachers and the priests are just giving you the word of God. Salvation is a gift. You can't earn it through your good works on this planet. Jesus said, "I am the way, the truth, and the life. No man cometh unto the Father, but by me."[4] So why is Jesus the only way to get to heaven? God doesn't want any man to boast.

Liberals have asked certain religious men/women if they will go to hell for not accepting Jesus as their lord and savior. If you are a Christian, then your belief makes you answer with: Unfortunately, the answer is yes. Then, they ask, will the ones who never learn about Jesus be given a second chance? Some Christians believe so. However, the ones who have been given the opportunity to learn about Jesus and choose some other religion, which looks good to the human perspective, will not go to heaven.

These other religions might make you spiritual, but unless you accept Jesus as your lord and savior, you won't get to heaven. So you liberal Democrats, if you want to know why, you will then have to wait until you die and stand in front of God, then you can ask Him why.

Have you ever noticed when you give the answer that good people don't go to heaven unless they accept Jesus Christ as their lord and savior? Liberal Democrats will say "how do you know" and "this is surely not fair"? Well, to the question of how do I know? The Bible tells me so. As to the second question about being unfair, you'll just have to take that up with Jesus when you see Him after you die. As a Christian, I cannot see into the hearts of people and be able to tell if they have accepted Jesus into their hearts, which will give them salvation.

Liberal Democrats that I have observed give me the impression that good should give way to evil. That no one is to be held accountable for his or her actions, except if you're a Christian, a conservative, or if you step outside their political correctness doctrine. That we the people of the United States don't have the right, to defend ourselves, unless we get permission through the United Nations or from the rest of the world.

What has happened to our Congress? They used to pass bills into laws based on strong Christian morals. They now seem to pass bills that become laws based on what is politically expedient for the politicians. When politicians pass laws for political reasons instead of what's good for the country, you get double standards, and we have a lot of those types of laws. Refer to chapter 9.

The Christian Way of Life

There are many non-Christians out there who will say, "Aren't Christians supposed to take care of the poor?" The answer to that question is that Christians are to help out the poor. Freeloaders are not the poor. They are people who feel someone should take care of them. The poor are not to be taken care of, as parents takes care of their children. Liberal Democrats don't seem to understand this concept. Liberal Democrats think that you should be willing to give all your money to them, and they will use it for the good of the world.

I don't think so. Communism doesn't work. There are a lot of examples out there; Russia for one. So how should we help the poor? The poor should be helped in a way that doesn't make them totally dependent on the federal government for survival. The Bible's Old Testament tells us how the poor should be helped and it is not through handouts. They are supposed to work for their food. It says those who do not work do not eat. The liberal Democrats of the United States tell me: the Old Testament doesn't apply to today's standards. Okay, so how do we help the poor? Surely not by handouts by our federal government, but maybe through charity where people give what they can afford to give, and not by having liberal Democrats take 40% of our money through taxes.

Jesus said the poor will always be among us, but He didn't say that we should become poor in the attempt to help them. He also said that you shouldn't horde your money. He wanted people to invest their wealth so it would create jobs, and to help support people through charity. Charity is voluntarily, it's giving up something you own and then giving it to another human being. Not being forced to do so. It's a shame that liberal Democrats don't understand this concept. Everyone is supposed to work.

Jesus was not a Liberal or a Conservative

I heard Alan Colmes' version of Jesus being a liberal Black man, supposedly backed up by scripture. I strongly disagree with his assessment. Not the Black man part, but Jesus was not a liberal or a conservative. Jesus was the son of God. I don't quite understand, why someone would argue over something as insignificant, as to what color Jesus Christ's skin was.

I have a hard time understanding some scriptures, and I don't go around quoting them or trying to put my own take to them. The bad thing about some people is that they can quote scripture from the Bible and haven't got a clue to what they're quoting. They quote scripture and take it out of context, to make it fit their point of view. You have to wonder why they are doing that.

Jesus didn't kick capitalists out of His Father's church. He kicked out people who were defiling His Father's temple. You sure they weren't liberal Democrats? These merchants were kicked out of the temple of God because they were cheating the people who brought animals in for sacrifice. By telling them that the animal was blemished and they needed to buy one of their animals. The people who came to the temple of God without an animal for sacrifice had to buy one, usually at double the cost, from one of the merchants in the temple of God. This animal was the same animal that the merchant called blemished, from the previous person who brought it in for his sacrifice. In other words, these merchants had a monopoly there. Something politicians like to create for themselves. Weren't politicians the ones who created our government monopolies? The next United States government monopoly they will create is health care.

If these merchants were fair in their pricing and the examination of the animals for sacrifice, Jesus would have left them alone. Not all capitalist's cheat people. If Jesus had something against capitalists, he would have run them off everywhere he went, which was not the case. The capitalists, who do cheat people, do get thrown into jail or punished some other way.

Liberal politicians, on the other hand, who cheat, deceive, connive, and lie, get protected by other liberal politicians in a position of power. Liberal politicians will find a way to protect their fellow colleagues or at least make up excuses for them to escape punishment.

Now if there were socialist Democrats there, as merchants, they would have had an entrance tax, a tax for the sacrificing of the animals, a tax for the weighing of the animal, a tax for using the scales for weighing the animal, a tax for using the altar while you sacrifice the animal to God, along with a property tax because you bought the animal, so it is your property. A tax for being there, a tax to pray to God, a tax for not praying to God, a tax for cleaning up after the sacrifice, a tax for not cleaning the altar if you choose not to sacrifice an animal. A tax if you did not sacrifice an animal, a tax for the priests, a tax for the merchants, a tax just to be taxed, a tax for the keeping of the books – after all, they have to know how many times you were there. A tax for the wear and tear on the temple of God, a tax for the deterioration of the altar, a tax for doing an impact study on the environment, a tax for walking in the temple of God, a tax for looking around the temple of God, a tax for talking to the merchants, a tax for wearing sandals in the temple of God, because walking in the temple of God with sandals on would aid in the deterioration of the temple. A tax for not wearing sandals in the temple of God, a tax for not talking to the merchants, a tax for not talking to the priests, a tax for talking to the priests, a tax for breathing while you were in the temple of God, a tax for worshiping God in the temple of God, a tax for not worshiping God in the temple of God and a tax for leaving the temple of God. This tax would amount to all the other taxes combined. This would ensure that the poor could sacrifice to God. As long as they know their place and allow these liberal socialists to keep on robbing the rich, as liberal Democrats so love to do. This would be called entitlements for the poor.

If there were animal rights activists there, then they would demand a stop to the animals being sacrificed to God. If there were environmental activists there, they would want an impact study done, to see what kind of damage would be done to the environment by animal blood. They would demand a stop to all sacrifices, until the impact on the environment would be known.

Jesus being a liberal Black man, I guess you can believe anything you want when it comes to Jesus' appearance, and if it brings you closer to God, more power to you, but I have read the Bible from cover to cover and I can't find anywhere in the Bible that states that Jesus was a Black man. I looked through the Bible to try to find, where it was stated, that Jesus had copper skin, red eyes and white hair, as some people have told me. I guess I will just have to wait until I die and see Jesus for myself, and then I will know for sure. Like that really matters to me if Jesus had black skin, white skin or copper skin. As far as Jesus being portrayed as a blonde-haired, blue-eyed White man, if it makes you feel better about yourself, then have at it. I have seen pictures with Jesus having blue eyes, which some Middle Eastern men have. It is extremely rare, and I wonder if the artist was trying to show that Jesus was an extremely rare individual. After all, there is only one Son of God, and that's Him.

Jesus was not a liberal or a conservative. Jesus doesn't want us to live our lives based on conservatism or liberalism. Jesus wants us to live our lives based on the example He set forth, while He was on this planet. Some people have tried to argue that Jesus was a liberal. While some others people have tried to argue that Jesus wasn't the Son of God. If it makes you feel good about yourself, more power to you,

It amazes me that people will argue over such an insignificant thing, such as, if Jesus Christ was a liberal or a conservative or was he Black, White or Oriental. What we should be doing, instead of arguing about Jesus being a liberal or conservative, Black, White, or Oriental, is we should be rejoicing in the fact that Jesus Christ is our lord and savior, which gives us the guarantee of a spot in heaven.

Jesus' life was not based on conservative or liberal ideals. Jesus' life was a testimony on how God wanted us to live our lives. Since we all have fallen short of what God has expected from us, He sent His only Son to die on the cross for our salvation. Jesus' blood has washed all our sins away, if we choose to believe in Him.

Jesus could not have been a liberal Democrat, because Jesus didn't believe in the murdering of unborn children or the euthanasia of the elderly. Jesus believed in the freedom of choice; something liberal Democrats have no concept of. Jesus never forced anyone to listen to Him. Either you believed or you didn't

I would like to know, where does it state in the Bible that Jesus believed in stealing? To be a liberal Democrat, you have to believe in stealing. A government that takes money from one group of people and then turns around and gives it to another group of people is stealing. No matter how you want to label it, it's still stealing. Jesus didn't believe in forcing someone to be charitable. Who do you see forcing charitable contributions? Most of the time, it's from liberal Democrats through taxation. Wasn't it Barack Obama who said, he wanted our money for the redistribution of wealth to be spread around to other people?

Jesus did state that it would be easier for a camel to pass through the eye of a needle, than for a rich man to make it to heaven. He also stated if you have two of something, then you should give one to your brethren. Jesus believed in a high moral standard of living, not the immoral way of life liberal Democrats and liberal organizations want you to live. Jesus didn't believe in gay sex, co-habitation, pre-marital sex, or any of the other perverse lifestyles we have today. Jesus said, live in the world but don't be of the world, for you surely will perish if you are.

Jesus believed that you should be held accountable for your actions. This is why he died on the cross for us. Salvation is a gift. I don't want to be standing next to anyone who asks Jesus to give him what he deserves. We cannot make it to heaven on our own.

Jesus did not believe in taking care of freeloaders or holding someone down, as liberal Democrats have with their social programs. So they can be used for someone's political agenda.

Jesus believed that people should work for their living. Where is the evidence for this statement that Jesus didn't believe in taking care of freeloaders? The Garden of Eden, for one, Adam didn't sit on his butt before he committed the same sin as Eve. He was supposed to take care of the garden. This means work the garden, and then he may eat some of the fruit. Jesus also was a carpenter before he started his ministry.

Did Jesus show any liberal tendency when he was alive? Once again, Jesus' life was a testimony to how God wanted us to live. Liberals have tried to say that Jesus was a liberal because he was a rebel and that he didn't work for a living, he just preached.

Preaching is a full-time job, in case some of you don't know that. There have been some exceptions, such as the Apostle Paul, who didn't want to be a burden to the people he was preaching to, and today with part-time ministers. But being a representative of God is a full-time job. That is why they draw a salary or an allowance. Some churches even give the pastor a place to live.

As far as Jesus being a rebel, to somebody's standard, He might appear as one, but that wasn't His purpose in life. His purpose was to save us from our sins and to give us the chance for eternal life with Him in heaven. He also set an example of how He wanted us to live.

I haven't found any writings in the Bible that would show Jesus as a liberal. Liberals try to say Jesus was a liberal because he cared for the people around him. Well, God loves everyone, but He will not drag you kicking and screaming into heaven. You have to accept Jesus Christ as your lord and savior and believe in your heart that Jesus is the Son of God.

Jesus is the Christ. You can't label him as a conservative or a liberal. He is the Son of God, which means if you believe in Him you will fall under the mercy of God. If you choose not to believe that Jesus is the Son of God, then you will fall under God's righteousness. I for one want to fall under God's mercy, not His righteousness. Falling under God's righteousness means He will judge me according to my works, which means that I will not go to heaven.

The big difference between Christianity and other religions is this: Other religions teach that you can get to heaven on your own by living a good life and by helping people in need, while the Christian religion teaches you that you can't get to heaven on your own, but only through the blood of Jesus Christ, can you make it.

So why do Christians try to do good things in their lives by helping others? That's easy. You try to live the life Jesus lived because you accepted Jesus Christ into your heart as your lord and savior. By accepting Jesus as your lord and savior, you try to do what Jesus would have done in the course of your travels.

Does God Still Have His Hands in His Creation?

Does God still play an active role in His creation? Yes, He does. Do we understand His will at all times? No, we don't. By not understanding His will, we cannot understand why He allowed certain people to become leaders of certain countries. When God allows an evil person to take a leadership role in a country, this doesn't mean He is not taking an active role in the history of the world.

People will ask me, how, could God allow Hitler to come into power and kill over 50 million people during his reign of terror. These same people will praise God for allowing Franklin Delano Roosevelt to be elected as President of The United States.

At all times do I understand God's will? No, I don't. If I understood God's will, at all times, then I would understand why He will allow the Anti Christ to take power over the world for seven years. So why does God allow bad things to happen in His creation? You will have to ask a theologian about that, or God when you die, but I will give you my opinion.

I believe it can be traced back to Adam and Eve. When Satan went to the weakest link in the chain of creation, he went and temped Eve, to eat some of the fruit God had forbidden them to eat. Even though Eve had eaten some of the fruit, her eyes were not open to the knowledge of good and evil because she was not the head of the household, but this started the ball rolling. She went to her husband and told him the same lie that was told to her, and also said that she did not die. When Adam, the head of the household, ate some of the forbidden fruit, their eyes became open to the knowledge of good and evil. By doing this, they told God that they didn't want His help or His teachings. They would decide to learn what is good and what is evil on their own. So God, who gave us free will, said okay.

This doesn't mean that God has taken a hand's off approach. When Adam and Eve's eyes were opened, God came to them and made them clothes, but also kicked them out of the Garden of Eden. He couldn't allow them to have eternal life in their corrupt state. He promised a savior would come and give them salvation. So God is a loving Father who will intervene when things get too bad for His people.

God will intervene when the Anti Christ takes power over the world by rapturing His people and taking them with Him to heaven. Has God intervened in the two darkest periods in our history? Some say yes and I don't know. When Jimmy Carter was President, he caused our country to become the laughingstock of the world. He ran our country into the ground with a 22% interest rate along with a 17% inflation rate. He also set out to destroy our military, which allowed Russia to invade Afghanistan.

So was Ronald Reagan God's intervention to the dark days of Jimmy Carter? I can't say that, but some people do. Jimmy Carter's solution to the invasion of Afghanistan was to boycott the Summer Olympics held in Russia. Reagan's solution was to set up groups of guerrilla fighters to engage the Russians, which caused Russia to suffer a war like we did in Vietnam. It took Reagan his first term to turn around Jimmy Carter's destruction, and then he gave us one of the greatest economies this country has ever seen.

The darkest period this country has ever suffered from was under the Clinton Years. When Bill Clinton was President of our country, he gave us one of the largest tax increases in the history of this country, or until Barack Obama became president. He destroyed our military, which led to the terrorist attacks on 9/11/2001. In his last year-and-a-half in office, he gave us a recession and according to Michael Savage, Bill Clinton gave us eight years of trickledown immorality. So is God intervening with Barack Obama? I don't think so. His presidency will be worse than Jimmy Carter's presidency. So will God intervene after Barack Obama's presidency, or will He let us suffer under another president such as Bill Clinton or Barack Obama?

Is it just me, or can other people see that when people walk a path, which takes them farther away from God. That their lives become more immoral and corrupt? Does this also happen when a nation's leaders, force their nation on a path that takes that nation farther away from God? Is this happening to the United States? When our nation was a Christian nation, it seems that we had a higher moral standard with less corrupt politicians. Or are we more open about it since we have become more of a secular nation? Has our path taken us so far away from God that He will not intervene for us any longer?

Liberalism

Chapter 18

So what is liberalism? Liberalism is the ability to go from one failure to the next with the charisma to blame someone else for those failures. Then proceed on with the same enthusiasm to your next failure, knowing full well that if you continue, you will eventually destroy your country, but not caring because your objective is to obtain power at any cost.

Liberals, it's hard to understand liberalism, considering that liberals govern their lives based on the feelings of the moment. Their decision making isn't must better because it is based on the same emotions that governs their lives. So why is it so hard to stay a liberal – or maybe better put, why is it so hard to stay a liberal once you develop a brain? Once your brain is developed and you see that humans are fallen beings, you start to realize that utopia can never be created by us.

You then realize that the world is not fair and never will be. This doesn't mean that you stop trying to make your life the best you can, but it does mean that you understand that you can't make the world fair. As someone put it to me, "The world is not fair because there are so many asses in charge of it." That statement got me thinking, and I finally realized what he was trying to say. We are all asses at any given time. So for the world to be fair, we would have to stop being asses. I don't see that happening anytime soon.

In the process of liberals trying to create utopia in our country, they had to come up with distortions of the facts. Yes, there are companies with people in charge that do hire and promote people based on friendship. It seems that we elect our servants based on popularity contests, not on facts or substance of character. Is this fair? No, it is not. Now, do all people get their jobs in the private sector based on friendship or popularity contests? No, they don't, but liberals want you to believe that. Most people when hired get their job based on experience, education, and being at the right place at the right time. In some cases, the right place at the wrong time.

Yes, I have seen people get promotions they didn't deserve. In some cases the person getting the promotion, who didn't deserve it, is the only one willing to take the job. He might have even gotten the promotion based on Affirmative Action. I have seen people who were deserving of a promotion and only got it to keep the person who didn't deserve a promotion out of trouble.

What other distortions have liberals come up with? They have come up with "The rich are getting richer and the poor are getting poorer." This statement is a half-true, and leaves out why this is happening. Big government is the main reason.

This situation came about by liberal Democrats trying to create utopia on Earth. In this effort of trying to create utopia, they have tried the redistribution of wealth. Has it worked? No, it hasn't, but they keep on trying, and in the process they have widened the gap between the rich and the poor. There are fundamental differences between these types of people, what makes one poor, middle class or rich. Liberals say that the only reason these people are poor is because of their circumstance or because of their environment.

When I was young, dumb, and naïve, I thought as most liberals think today, that to level the playing field, we have to empower our federal government to take money away from the ones working hard for their living, and give it to people who either don't want to work or don't have the education for a well-paying job.

I have noticed that during every presidential campaign, the liberal Democrat running for office has lowered the tax base line on the rich, which he is going to raise taxes on. The money from this tax increase is supposed to go to the poor.

Why do they have to levy higher taxes on a greater amount of people in the United States? It is because the money they need to level the so-called playing field becomes greater every year. This is because their policies have created more poor people instead of leveling the playing field. Spreading the wealth around doesn't work. What they really are doing is spreading misery around, and more and more people are falling into it. Beware of liberal Democrats. They will deceive you every chance they get. Remember what the Bible says: Make sure no man deceives you.

The middle class in the United States is almost wiped out, due to liberal Democrats trying to redistribute the wealth. No matter how they spin it, they can't get the money they want out of the rich. They have to go to the middle class to get this money. So what's happening to us, the middle class? Our tax burden gets higher our savings get smaller, and more of us slip into the ranks of the poor. If we continue in this manner, we will have the poor, the extremely poor, the rich, and the extremely rich.

The politicians in the United States will be the extremely rich because as always, they will exempt themselves from the laws they pass. Why do I think this way? Some of the wealthiest people in the United States run our federal government.

Circumstances and Environments

It is interesting to me, and some of this might be true: circumstances and environments do play a part in one's life. A lot of people have become rich, and they have come out of the ranks of the poor and middle class, but these people weren't afraid of hard work. They had dedication and discipline, a goal they wanted to achieve, and a desire to make it in the world. They didn't think that the federal government was going to come along and give it to them.

Giving people money, does it improve their situation? I would have to say no. Has welfare improved the situation of the people receiving this money? Have their lives improved or are they living in the same conditions as before? They're living in the same situation. They're just being paid to stay there. So one needs to ask, if welfare has done very little in the way of helping these people get out of the ranks of the poor. What would do it? Would hard work do it? Would an education do it? Would getting the federal government off their backs do it? Would getting politicians to stop holding them back do it?

I believe all of these are needed. You have a God-given right in this world, which is the right to compete. Now I know that liberals hate competition. They are trying everything they can to kill competition in their government-run schools, from school vouchers to home schooling and competitive sports. If you choose to listen to them and choose not to compete, that is your decision, but I shouldn't be held accountable for your decision.

When you get out of school, you will find yourself in a competitive environment, which you will have to compete in, or become a slave to the federal government and go on welfare. When I got out of school, I chose to compete. I might not compete as well as some, but that's what I chose. So I don't like it when someone comes up to me and says that we have to empower our federal government, to take money away from those who have worked hard all of their lives, and give it to someone else in our society.

Most of the time, the one making this claim is a person who doesn't want to work for his achievements, he wants them given to him. This is funny, in a way, because anytime you are given something you have a tendency not to take care of it. You feel that the person or persons, who gave you this, will just give you another one. If you want an example, just look at your children, how they will take care of something that was given versus earned. I also want the destiny that God has chosen for me, not have the federal government choose it for me.

So then, what is my responsibility to the offspring of our generation? This is interesting to me, when this question is asked. The answer is that we as a society have an obligation to our offspring, to give them the tools necessary to compete in this world. What are these tools? We have to give them an education or job skills, which will give them the ability to find and obtain a good paying job.

Now, an education is needed in this country. You use to be able to find a decent paying job in the manufacturing industries, but due in part to our federal government and state governments, running the manufacturing industries out of the United States. We now have high school educated people finding jobs that give them, dead-end careers and low pay.

So the question needs to be asked: Are we providing the necessary tools to our offspring, so they can make it in this world? The answer is no. Our education system needs to be revamped. I like the Japanese style of education. The finest minds, the students who work hard at getting decent grades, go to the best schools and pay very little for their education. The students who are lazy that don't work hard and gets poor grades, go to the schools of lesser quality and pays for it. We need to start to instill in our young. The realization that they will be competing in this world in everything they do.

By giving the students who achieve an award, this will give them a desire to achieve and to study harder. The award in Japan is to go to a school that they wouldn't be able to afford. The rich family and the poor family have the same opportunity. The rich family can't use their power, to get their lazy son or daughter in the best schools.

I realize that some can, and most of these parents are politicians, but I also realize that the world isn't fair. As a whole, the ones with the best grades go to the best schools, in Japan. So why haven't we developed this system of education? Is it because the rich don't want their children to compete for these spots? Is it because under the Japanese system of education, you won't be beholden to someone who gives you a scholarship, because you made it there on your own, with the help of your teachers? I wonder if this is why teachers in the Oriental countries are held in such high esteem, by their students.

I know what some people think, that this lazy person might come out of it and actually be a better worker than the hard-working student. That is the case sometimes, but it is rare. If this were common, we wouldn't be getting our ass handed to us by the Japanese in the business and the manufacturing worlds. How many of you will buy an American-made car over a Japanese-made car?

So if the answer is no, we are not giving our offspring the necessary tools to make it in this world, then we need to ask why. Do we have a poor education system? If so, what do we need to do about it?

Liberal Democrats say spend more money on it. Most of the money we spend on education goes to the teachers and the building of the infrastructure. Teachers are protected by a union, so bad teachers can't be fired. If we put more money into our education system, the money will go to the teachers and the infrastructures of the schools. Very little will go toward buying the education supplies needed to educate our offspring.

I realize that teachers need to have a decent salary to live on, but some accountability needs to come with that job. Are the teachers in our government-run school system doing a good job of educating the children? Some are and some are not, but as long as these teachers who are doing their jobs poorly continue to teach the liberal doctrine. They will be protected by their unions and liberal politicians. This needs to be changed.

Throwing money at a problem is always the answer to a liberal Democrat, which is why we are in the shape we're in, but that's another chapter. Throwing money at a problem is not always the answer. It's an easy way out. It makes people think you are doing something about the problem, but as always with the liberal Democrat way of handling a problem, nothing gets resolved. The true answer is: we need to get rid of the liberal utopianism doctrine, which is being taught in our government-run schools. Another factor is that liberals refuse to correct our children in school when they make a mistake. They have taken out discipline so that unruly children will be drugged into submission instead of implementing a program of discipline. Which one is better?

Discipline is better. Yes, you can destroy someone's spirit if you over-discipline them. Drugging someone into submission will destroy their spirit and possibly give them a drug addiction. Do liberal politicians hope for this? I think they do. If you have someone who can't make it in the real world, they will need federal government assistance. This will justify government programs and keep them running. So destroying the lives of our children by giving them a poor education, is done, to justify the existence of federal government employees, which will allow them to keep their jobs.

Liberal teachers are more into the feel good scenario than the education scenario. If you are not shown your mistakes, then how will you know what is correct? Once you get into the real world, you will make mistakes. How you handle them will determine if you keep a job or not. One way to learn is to make mistakes and then learn from them. In other words, you don't do them again. Sometimes you have to be shown the mistake, you made, to learn from it. Never being shown your mistakes will make you indecisive and unsure of yourself when you are confronted with your mistake. It might make you unwilling to try again, in fear of making another mistake. In your life, you're going to make mistakes. If you are afraid of making a mistake and refuse to do your job, you will get fired. Learning to work through your mistakes is needed at a young age. This should be part of your education in school.

Liberals need to recruit victims so they can stay in power. What better way than to have an uneducated person living below his/her potential? Is this why we have such a poor education system? Do we have a poor education system because of the laziness of the parents of our offspring? Do we have a poor education system due to the punitive tax system we have in this country? Do we have a poor education system in this country because both parents are working? Do we have a poor education system in this country because of single moms? We have a poor education system because we as a society haven't taken the time to correct it, and the liberal politicians have capitalized on this situation.

Liberal Utopia

How is raising taxes on the wealthy going to create utopia? It's not, but liberals don't want any facts to get in the way of their utopian legislation. This is amazing to me. They usually exempt themselves from their legislation. Then, after they exempt themselves from it, they turn around and promote said legislation, by saying it is unfair to our children or to the poor if we don't pass this legislation.

If we want to talk about unfairness, is it fair for someone to exempt themselves from these so-called fairness laws? These fairness laws don't fix the problems. They only spread misery to a greater number of people, living in the United States. We do need to stop being so envious of our fellow citizens who have made it. You haven't made it because you haven't tried.

So why do we allow liberal Democrats to spread misery around? Misery loves company. Someone who is miserable can't stand it if someone is doing well. He has to try to get this person down to his level, and if he can empower our federal government to do it for him, then that's even better.

Have you noticed that the people talking about fairness are usually wealthy politicians? Ted Kennedy is one example. Has any of his legislation, which has become law, helped in leveling the playing field? Has it gotten rid of any of this so-called unfairness in our society? I believe his legislation has inflamed the situation, but if you can put the blame on someone or something else, you can create a power base for yourself by acting like you care about the unfairness in the United States.

It is nothing new for politicians to launch attacks on the wealthy. The Greeks tried the same thing back in Plato's days. The rich Greeks got tired of the community they were living in, stealing their money through the legal means of taxation. So they fled to a nearby community that took them in and gave them political asylum. Naturally, the people who were living off these rich people through taxation wanted the community, which was harboring them, to return them. War was threatened by these mooches and did occur when that community refused to appease them. The freeloaders lost and the rich stayed where they were.

When our tax burden gets too high, will we have people leaving the United States? This is what happened in Canada, but it wasn't the rich that left, it was the middle class. Where do we go when our federal government becomes as oppressive, and our taxes reach 70% to 80%, especially when nations around us are just as oppressive? There are a lot of rich people leaving our country, so liberal Democrats are getting upset by the number of companies going offshore to get work done. Will the freeloaders in our society try to persuade our federal government to go to war, to get their meal tickets back? I don't know, but we are seeing companies leave in record numbers.

So what's the answer to keep companies in the United States? The answer liberal Democrats give is – this shouldn't be a surprise to you – we should raise their taxes as punishment for getting work done outside the United States. The reason why American companies are getting work done outside the United States is so they can compete. One other way of saying this, is they get work done outside the United States, because their tax burden is so high that they can't compete against other companies, which have their country's government helping them, with taxes incentives.

So what should be done? Lower the tax burden on these companies that want to do business in the United States. Since we are living in a global community and companies can go anywhere in the world to do business, raising their taxes isn't the answer. The raising of taxes, to punish these companies for leaving, won't work. They will just move their global headquarters to the country where they have the work done. Is this why the federal government took over Chrysler and GM?

Let's give these companies incentives to compete in the global community here in the United States, which will keep jobs here. So how do we make them more competitive? Regulations and taxes are killing our companies' competitiveness.

I personally don't think that lowering salaries will make them more competitive. The people in the United States have a hard enough time making it now. If you don't pay your talented people, they will go somewhere else in this global community.

Will lowering their taxes help? Yes, I believe that will help. Will it help by giving these companies new buildings with new technologies? Yes, as long as we have people who have been educated or trained on how to use these new technologies.

Will breaking up the unions help? I have always wondered why people from the same country who have worked for Honda, Toyota and Nissan can produce a car the people of the United States want and have pride in the ownership of, while Ford, Chrysler and GM have such a hard time at it.

Is this because of the unions or poor management on the part of these companies? I believe it is both. The unions protect their members even if they can't do the job, don't want to do the job, or are too lazy to do the job, but they expect their members to get paid for being there. Union members can't be fired for not working or for insubordination. They can only be fired for offenses that are agreed upon in the contract. Unions are good examples of socialism (liberalism).

Has mismanagement occurred in these manufacturing companies? Why of course. When did this start? It started when these companies put bean counters in the CEO positions. You probably want some examples, but first, bean counters can be CEOs of companies that are not manufacturing-based, and they probably would do a good job. Now, manufacturing-based companies need an individual who understands the manufacturing techniques of products, not accounting or finances. People who understand accounting and finances should be hired for that part of the business, but never have the final say on how a manufacturing business should be run. Bean counters in manufacturing businesses usually make the wrong decisions.

Ford, Chrysler and GM started their downward decline in the market in the 1970s, due to poor workmanship and by misreading the markets. The energy crisis didn't help matters. People wanted nice-looking, fuel-efferent cars. The big three didn't have any of these types of cars, but the Japanese car manufactures did. So what did the U.S. car manufactures do to stop the bleeding? Nothing they just sat back and complained about the situation.

It seems we do a lot of that these days. Have we become a nation of do-nothing complainers? We have a lot of people in this country who are good at complaining. The automobile manufacturers, through their complaining, tried to get the United States federal government to levy tariffs. Were bean counters running Ford, Chrysler and GM? I believe they were.

Legislating Utopia

What utopian legislation have we passed in the last forty years, and what are the causes of this legislation? Most if not all of this type of legislation has not worked. What has LBJ's Great Society done, besides destroying the family structure of our society? What has his welfare programs done? It has made a section of our society lazy and dependent on the federal government. Recipients of welfare have put on the noose of government slavery. Refer to chapter 4.

If you are waiting on the government to pull you out of the situation you are in, you are going to have a long wait. Most liberal politicians want you dependent on them. That way, you become a member of their party and will vote the way they tell you to vote. If they allow you off one of their programs, then they lose you as a member of their party. I hope you are enjoying that form of slavery.

Another form of federal government enslavement is taxes. If you don't pay your taxes, you are going to see jail time, unless you are a Timothy Geithner. Pete Rose and Wesley Snipes got jail time. Why are politicians like Timothy Geithner exempted from jail time? Is this fair? No, but he's a liberal Democrat elitist. Laws don't apply to him.

If you use the programs, the federal government has put in place to improve your life, on your own. You are more likely to make it in this cruel unfair world we live in, than waiting on the federal government of the United States. The federal government programs designed to help you make it in this world would be student loans to go to college, or business loans to start a small business. If you can get a school scholarship, your chances of success are even greater, as long as you apply yourself. Where the problem lies to these federal government programs is: you do have to work for it. You can't go to college and flunk out or start a small business and have someone else run it for you. Both of these efforts require hard work, dedication, and a desire to achieve. These are the traits that will make you rich, not sitting on your butt, waiting for the federal government.

Now the first utopian legislation was passed back in the 1930s. One of these was called Social Security. This is where the federal government decided that it had the right to force companies and people, to put a certain amount of money away into a federal government-run trust fund. Refer to chapter 1.

Was Social Security a good idea? Yes, but all liberal ideas are good ideas. They just don't work or have the desired results. If you raise an objection to these money-sucking, never-ending programs, you are labeled mean-spirited. If we would just take a step back for a moment and ask ourselves this question: What right do we have to someone else's money? Then maybe we would stop empowering our federal government, to pass legislation to steal someone else's money.

Most of these people work hard for their money and most conservatives give large sums of money to charity. So they're not mean-spirited people. If you look at the charitable contribution of liberals, like Joe Biden, you will see he didn't even give 1% of his salary to charity.

This is one of the differences between liberals and conservatives. Liberals believe in empowering the federal government, while conservatives believe in empowering the people. Which one is better? If you believe in empowering people, they will be able to stand on their own. If you believe in empowering our federal government, you will need to pay more taxes down the road. Then our federal government will also need to find someone else in need, so they can keep their power. This is one reason why our federal government regulates problems and never solves problems.

So what are some of the good ideas that liberals have that don't have the desired results, they were supposed to bring into our world? Here's a few: Social Security, prescription drugs for the elderly, Medicare for the elderly, HMO insurance for the poor, and Medicaid for the poor. All of these programs except for HMO are about bankrupt. That means more taxes have to be collected.

You see, these are good ideas until you ask the question: Who's going to pay for all of this? In spite of class envoy, which liberal Democrats have tried to instill in people, the rich can't pay for all of these federal government programs. If the liberals try to get the rich to pay for all their federal government programs, the economy will suffer and they might just leave the country.

So here's where the middle class comes into the picture and why the middle class is slowly being removed from our society. There was another superpower that wiped out their middle class for about 200 years, and that was China. China's middle class has finally started to re-emerge. If we don't want, what happened to China's middle class, to happen to us, we better look at how they wiped out their middle class and learn from it.

So what are the answers liberal Democrats give, when they are told that all of the utopian bills they have passed into law, haven't worked? Their answer is that more money needs to be spent on them or new ones need to be created. What we really need to do is eliminate these utopian laws and create laws that help people stand on their own two feet. Let's not try to create utopia, but a country that educates its people so good paying jobs can be obtained.

The Black Hole of Liberalism

We as a society need to ask ourselves: Do we really want to throw our money into this black hole, which will suck up our money but provide very little in desired results? Usually the money spent on big government wasteful social programs produces very little, in comparison to the money it takes to run them. In other words, it's a bad deal.

If we move into liberalism, we as a nation need to be concerned and make sure we don't fall into communism. We need to really think this over. One nation that was a staunch believer in communism has been slowly moving away from that type of government. They started a slow but steady shift from communism to capitalism. Their first step in their progression was to implement a capitalistic economy. Although they are still looked upon as a Communist nation by the world, China has made strives to move from communism to capitalism.

China has come a long way since 1949. Today China is a world economic power. They are an industrial, agricultural and export power. This achievement was based on their move to a capitalistic economy, or was it because they are rapidly moving to a Christian society?

God said that He would bless His people. Was it Christianity that caused China's leaders to ease up on their persecution of their people? Did Christianity make them realize that a more tolerant approach was needed in their country? Secularists will say capitalism did it, while Christians might say God did it. I think it was God, who used capitalism as His tool to bring prosperity to China.

If the above statement is true, which I believe it is, then why are we allowing the United States to slip into a socialistic form of government and an atheist form of a society? Is this happening because we have allowed the liberal atheists that run our country, to implement their intolerance to anyone who disagrees with their perverse lifestyle?

What are we thinking of, why are we moving from a capitalistic economy to a liberalistic economy? We need to ask, is it better to live in a country with a communist form of government that has a capitalistic economy, or a country that has a republic form of government with a communistic economy? The best form of government to me is a republic. The best form of an economy would be a capitalistic economy.

I have been to China six times in the last ten years, and I would have to say that I haven't seen much difference between the United States and China. In fact, as long as you obey the laws of any country you visit, you won't have any problems. People in China go about their everyday living just as we do. They go to work and come home; sometimes they go out to eat. They raise their child, as we raise our children, except that their children still have respect for their elderly and their parents. Their culture is different than ours, and I would have to say that I like their culture better.

As I said, there isn't much difference between our country and China. Now that being said, which country would I rather live in? Unfortunately, I would have to say China, for right now. There are two reasons I say this. China is moving away from communism and moving to capitalism. They are moving away from atheism and toward tolerance to Christianity.

By China moving away from their communistic ways and moving to a capitalistic form of government, they will start to realize that Christianity is truly a peaceful religion and will allow it to take root in their country. By doing this, they have increased my desire to live there. I just hope I can get there before the United States refuses to allow its people to leave. When that happens, I will know that the United States has fully embraced communism.

China still has a ways to go, but they will get there. When I was in China, I would ask the people I was visiting if they thought they would see free elections in their lifetime. They all said no, but they thought that their children would. So with that being the case, why are liberal Democrats becoming as oppressive as the Communist leaders in China, in the 1950s? Why do liberal Democrats want to control every aspect of our everyday life? Is it because liberal Democrats are power hungry? I have found it interesting, to talk to liberal Democrats in general, even though they get quite violent or just start calling you names when you break down their augments with logic.

You see liberal Democrats, have to live in the moment. That way history starts anew when they wake up in the morning. Nothing they do is subject to history. This is why welfare and all the other monster programs are not a failure to them. Welfare, Social Security, Medicare, Medicaid, food stamps and the prescription drug program just need more money spent on them. After all, these programs that do very little in the way of help need to be there. Why? Well, they just do.

Liberals Have Diarrhea of the Mind

Liberals, are they brain dead? I don't know some might be. Some people think that liberalism is a mental disorder, Michael Savage, for one. I believe that the bleeding heart liberals have a mental disorder but just liberals, themselves, don't. They have a naiveté that makes anyone who has developed a brain think they are suffering from a mental disorder. They believe in appeasement. They think that if they give tyrants and dictators what they want, everything will be all right afterwards.

Can anyone tell me, of an instance, where appeasement has worked? Appeasement is looked upon as a weakness by tyrants and dictators. It only emboldens them. Appeasement didn't work with Hitler. It won't work with the dictators we have in the world today, but liberal Democrats don't seem to understand this. This might be why some think they have a mental disorder.

I think bleeding heart liberals have cerebral diarrhea. They can't fathom that people won't see appeasement as trying to get along with someone. They don't understand why it is looked upon as a weakness. They can't understand that people who have worked hard all their lives don't want to give their hard-earned money to freeloaders and moochers. They can't understand why some people want to live by some established moral foundation.

Liberals don't look into the past to see if anything can be learned by it. If they did look into the past, they would have seen that appeasement has been tried many times and it has failed every time.

Yes, I know that liberals quote history, but they never seem to put into practice, the lessons we should have learn from it.

Why do liberals refuse to implement lessons of history, we should have learned from? I don't know. Could it be that they really can't learn from past events and just put on a good show? Some examples of events that we should have learned from but haven't are Korea, Vietnam, Somalia, appeasement of Hitler, and appeasement of every dictator from 1980, up until today.

So why do I think that liberals have cerebral diarrhea? People who use their brain and rationally think things through very seldom come up with disasters. The people, who brainstorm and come up with great ideas, have their ideas pass the scrutiny of others and time. Some people brainstorm and have cerebral drizzle, which usually, doesn't make it past the scrutiny of others, but when liberals brainstorm, they have cerebral diarrhea.

So how do they get their ideas put into law? They use their favor ploys! They start off with the strategy of class warfare and then they go into the scare tactics along with the "it's good for our children" routine. Hitlerisms are used. They will tell you, lie after lie until you start to believe it. How do you think Barack Obama got elected? They also try to put you on the defensive, to keep you from discussing the issues. All of these strategies have worked in the past and will work in the future. So we need to be aware of them and ask ourselves is it true or just liberal cerebral diarrhea?

There are three observations I have made, when I have discussed political issues with liberals and they are: Liberals don't want any hard questions put to them. If you do question their argument, by stating facts, which they don't have an answer for, they start calling you names. If calling you names doesn't get you to back off, they become physically violent. I would think that since I'm a rational thinking being that if you want me to go along with you, you need to be able to present a rational idea, not just some emotional half-witted idea that will cost a lot of money, time and effort, and in the long run won't work.

The three ploys liberals use that are the most effective are class warfare, destroying your character, and putting you on the defensive. If you don't think that class warfare is effective, then you need to read history and view the historical records of the 1930s, where Germany used class warfare against the Jews. If liberals can destroy your character, they feel people won't listen to you.

Why is putting you on the defensive so effective? It is effective because you can't debate the issue at hand. You are too busy telling people that you're not what the liberals say you are. You don't have the opportunity and time to explain that the plan liberals have come up with is bad, for the people and the country. So why do they use these tactics? I believe they are afraid of debate, which is why they try to destroy their challengers' character, or at least put them on the defensive.

When you disagree with a liberal, you are suddenly a racist, a homophobe, a sexist, you don't care about the welfare of our children or the elderly, and you are arrogant and egotistical. You are the most vile, evil, nastiest human being on the face of the Earth. Another reason these tactics are used is so people won't express their opinion along with their views, in fear of being verbally attacked.

I think liberals want you to be afraid of being verbally attacked by them. If they can make you fear them by attacking and destroying your character, you won't voice your concerns about liberal cerebral diarrhea legislation.

Why don't liberals want facts to enter into the issues? If facts did enter into the issues, they wouldn't get any of their ideas put into law. When's the last time a liberal was truthful to the people of the United States and told us what he/she really stood for? What his/her true ideas were? I believe the last time this occurred was when Walter Mondale was running for President of the United States.

I don't hear the truth from liberal Democrats anymore, so why should I vote for them? I just hear name calling and questions about someone's character, distortion of the facts, and blaming their opponents for everything that has gone wrong. I never hear what they stand for or how to fix what's wrong. You have to figure that out for yourself.

What are some examples of liberals having cerebral diarrhea? Well, how about their ideas on the prisoner of war system? They want to bring terrorists to our country's prisons and try them as if they were United States citizens. How about their ideas on the system of law in general? Laws should apply to us the commoners, but not to the liberal Democrat elites. How about their ideas on the health care system? They refuse to look at other nations that have tried their form of health care. It doesn't work, and they refuse to learn from that.

Why I Am Not a Liberal

Why I'm not a liberal. Well, I don't have the Emperor or Empress mentality. I don't think laws should be passed for everyone to obey but me. I don't tell half-truths, I don't distort the facts or spin facts in a way to cause deception. I don't believe in class warfare to divide a nation. I don't believe in keeping the people of the United States ignorant so they remain Democrats. I can't overlook that liberals feel that their agenda should come first, even at the cost of our nation. I don't believe that the solution to every problem in our country is more federal government intrusion into our society, and higher taxes to pay for every regulation they come up with. I don't believe in their efforts to solve the nation's problems by taking away our freedoms under the disguise of "it's good for the well being of the children and our country."

One reason I'm no longer a Democrat is because I believe the Democratic Party has lost its way. It was the party of the working man/woman, but now it's the party of any extremist group that can get them elected. An example would be their picking up the banner for illegal immigrants. The Democratic Party is also a collection of special interest groups which have formed an alliance, with each group supporting each other, with their main purpose being to grow government.

The second reason I'm not a liberal Democrat is because I don't believe that some people are above the law. What liberals feel they're above the law? How about Bill Clinton? The "independent prosecutor had enough to prosecute" him, so why didn't he? [1] Tom Daschle is another example of a liberal who must feel he is above the law. He has made millions of dollars in the private sector, but failed to pay $128,203 in taxes. Now he said he made a mistake, but I wonder if he would have paid his fair share, if he hadn't gotten a call from Barack Obama. No one knew of Tom Daschle's mistake, until he was offered a cabinet position by Barack Obama. When the scrutiny got too intense, "Tom Daschle withdrew" his name "as President Barack Obama's nominee to be health and human services secretary."[2]

The third reason is because liberals distort facts. When Tom Daschle was in public life, did he try to distort the facts, to persuade people to go along with his way of thinking? He tried to discredit the Republicans so the people of the United States would make a serious error and vote for the Democratic Party, during election years. I believe a majority must have believed him, because one of the biggest mistakes we made was to elect Barack Obama as our president.

Here is one of his distorted statements: "'Bush's tax cuts probably made the recession worse." [3] Does he really believe that we would fall for that? After all, we were living under the Clinton's Presidency for eight years and the recession started in the last year-and-a-half of his second four-year term in office.

Has the stimulus bill that Barack Obama signed into law helped our economy, or has it caused our recession to worsen? I believe it has caused our recession to worsen, and if it is not stopped, we will go into a depression.

The fourth reason is because liberals tell half-truths. To be a liberal, you must be able to tell a half-truth with a straight face. A good example is this: "the rich aren't paying their fair share." This statement is right, the rich aren't paying their fair share – they are paying more than their fair share, but this part is left out. When liberals make their half-truth statements, especially the one above, this is to start class warfare. The rich that I'm writing about aren't politicians, who can manipulate the system and pay nothing.

If this doesn't show that the rich are paying more than the fair share, nothing will: "according to data from the Internal Revenue Service."[4] "The top 1 percent of income earners pays nearly 35 percent of the income tax burden; the top 10 percent pay 65 percent; and the top 25 percent pay nearly 83 percent."[5] "The bottom 50 percent of income earners, on the other hand, pays barely 4 percent of income taxes."[6] "By definition, then, it is impossible to cut taxes without the so-called rich receiving a share of the benefits."[7]

The fifth and final reason is because liberals use class warfare to get what they want. In my opinion, class warfare is a must to liberal Democrats, and they achieve this through creating racial tension, through half-truths, and by putting the rich and the poor at odds with each other. The middle class falls in there as their tax base.

Why would they do this? Well, divide and conquer comes to my mind. If you don't believe me, the first people to point out how the rich are taking advantage of the poor, are liberal Democrats. It's not true, but they say it. Who are the ones who say the rich are getting richer and the poor are getting poorer? This is another half-truth to infuriate the people who aren't rich. The other half of this statement should be that, when the rich have money invested into stocks or bonds, the interest alone will make them richer, if they allow it to compound. Poor people can't invest their money. They use their money just to survive, while the investments of the middle class can eventually put them into the rich category, or keep them at their current levels.

The above examples of half-truths are also done to divert your attention away from them and onto someone else. That way they can pass laws or get re-elected without you knowing what they are doing. This brings to light the old saying, "out of sight, out of mind."

How a True Liberal Thinks

Here is how a true liberal thinks: he is successful at whatever he/she is doing. He/she feels guilty for being successful, so he/she runs for public office, probably under the Democratic Party, to make sure no one will be as successful as he/she is. He/she gets laws passed, to tax people for being successful. He/she then will exempt himself/herself from the tax. He/she takes the money and gives it to a poor person, so they may become successful. Instead the poor person takes the money to buy food to feed his family. This makes the liberal Democrat feel righteous. Then from his feeling of righteousness, he will raise your tax even higher, to help support the poor person. This is called helping the disadvantaged.

Another example of how a liberal thinks is this: two men are having a dual. They mark off ten paces and then come back to the starting point. They start back to back and start to walk away from each other, until the ten paces are up, but one man turns early and fires his weapon, wounding the other. The wounded man recovers his position and returns fire, killing his opponent. Now if liberal Democrats were backing the man who was killed, the liberal Democrats would say that man shot his opponent, who had an unloaded gun and should be punished for such an act. The liberal Democrat news media outlets, the lackeys of the Democratic Party, would jump on the bandwagon with articles supporting the claim of the liberal Democrats. When in reality, the one who turned and fired early should be the one punished for such an act, if he had lived.

The Definition of a Liberal by Webster's Dictionary

If you look up the definition of a liberal by the ***Webster's Dictionary***, you will see a grandiose over-exaggeration of an explanation, of a way of thinking or being. In fact, most liberals will quote the definition by verse. I told you, what I think the true meaning of liberalism really is, in my opening paragraph of this chapter, not what the dictionary will give you, but let's look at the definition of a liberal.

The definition of a liberal says that they are "favorable to progress or reform as in political or religious affairs."[8] If this means they are in favor of rewriting our Constitution to agree with their political correctness agenda, then that part of the definition fits. If it means, they want our nation to hold a policy like Russia and become a Godless nation, than that part also fits. Another part of the definition of a liberal is that they are "generous and are willing to give in large amounts." This is true, providing that it is someone else's resources. [9]

Being generous with their own resources is the furthest thing from their minds. They spend your money, not theirs. How do you think the statement tax-guzzling Democrat got started? It got started from people who keenly realize what a Democrat really is, a spendthrift, tax-guzzling liberal that looks at the middle class and the wealthy in the United States as a tax base. When they want to spend more money, they simply raise your taxes.

Tax Cuts that Really Mean Tax Increases

One of Bill Clinton lies during his 1992 Presidential election campaign, was he was going to lower our taxes. What he really wanted to say was: I need more money to spend, so I'm going to raise your taxes and cut military spending. Barack Obama promised a tax cut for 95% of the people making less than $250,000 per year, and he has cut military spending. I believe we did get the tax cut. It shows up as $8 to $15 a week on our paychecks. George Bush 41 tried this during his recession. Did it work?

When I was in college, unemployment was tax-free up until the Jim Carter's Presidency, who, in case someone doesn't remember, made unemployment taxable, but only if it put you over $20,000 per year in wages. Now, in today's society, under the liberal Democrat's direction, unemployment is 100% taxable.

During the Ronald Reagan Presidency, Reagan wanted to restructure our tax system. How many of you remember when Dan Rostenkowski, the Chairman of the House Ways and Means Committee, got on television after Reagan's State of the Union address? He said that he and his Democratic Party were going to do more than Reagan wanted. They were going to close the loopholes on the tax forms, so the rich wouldn't be able to use them when filing their taxes. This will help the poor. "It took the hard fight for the loophole-closing Tax Reform Act of 1986 to curb the tax shelters and abuses that the 1981 act created."[10] Well, he closed them all, but it hurt the middle class and the poor more than the rich.

How is this? They closed off the deductions (loopholes) on credit card interest, interest on car loans and on sales tax. If they really want to help the middle class and the poor, they should have done a maximum deduction for these items, say $1,500. Now that would have helped us and would have given them more tax dollars from the rich. Class envy got us again.

As I tell everyone that I meet when a discussion on politics comes up, "Do you really believe that a rich person is going to pass a tax law, which will give you a break and puts more of a burden on him/her?" Most of the time, I get asked a question before he/she answers the question. One of these questions is, "What do you mean"? Well, most of the United States Congress consists of rich men and women.

One of the powers of the House of Representatives is to start bills, which can become laws, providing that the Senate passes them and the President signs them into law.

Do you really think that they will pass a law that will give you tax relief? They usually give me this answer: "The Republicans do." Yes, Republicans do, but liberals just recently got control of the House and the Senate again, and the first words out of their mouths were: We must raise taxes. Though the Republicans under George Bush's Presidency got us a tax cut, liberals under Barack Obama's Presidency want to take away our tax cut.

Who is the most efficient with spending their money, the people of the United States or the federal government of the United States? Surely not the federal government, for the longest time they couldn't balance a budget of $1.6 trillion. Their budget today is $3.5 trillion, with deficit spending of $1.8 trillion, making it $5.3 trillion, give or take a few hundred billions here or there.

The only reason the government budget got balanced under the Bill Clinton's Presidency is because of the Republican Party. The Republican Party, for the first time in 40 years, in the 1994 election, gained the majority in both bodies of Congress and forced Bill Clinton to take a more aggressive deficit reduction plan.

Typical Liberalism

Conservatives will have to educate the unions or some of the rank and file members. The union member I have talked to, all tell me that we have to keep a certain amount of people on welfare, so they can get a dollar or two more on the hour. This is typical liberalism. I want a good salary and the hell with everyone else. Some of these people call themselves Christians.

These people say that the more people you put into the workforce would bring more competition to their job market, which would cause them to compete for these jobs. This in turn means less money. My reply to them is: I thought that you belong to a union, which would mean that these people would have to belong to your union, before they could possibly work at that company you work for, which would mean they would get the same pay as you get.

Do they actually believe that some people should be kept down in our society to where they barely can exist, instead of living, so they can earn more money? I believe so. I believe they don't want these people to join their union and these people could only join their union if more workers were needed.

Maybe this is what they're afraid of when the economy is in a boom period. Everyone is working, and their union might need more people to join, to help ease the workload. However, after the economic boom is over and an economic slowdown starts to occur, they might feel they will have to compete for jobs.

This to me still doesn't make sense. Why? I do know that being a member of a union, seniority is used for layoffs. The one with the most seniority is the last to be laid off. When it comes to pay, I do know that when you receive your journeyman's card, you get the same amount of pay. It doesn't matter how much experience and education you have. However, this might only apply to the building trades.

Liberals are rewriting Our Constitution

As I was watching the Hannity and Colmes TV news hour one night, to get both sides of the issues, they had Walter E. Williams on. What Mr. Williams had said was rather interesting. The United States federal government was intruding into our society more than our founding fathers wanted them to. He said that our forefathers had given the federal government limited powers that they were exceeding. In his interpretation of the Constitution, the federal government was taking too much power away from the states and making the federal government the centralized power, which was not what our founding fathers wanted.

Here's where I differ with Walter E. Williams. He says the United States federal government, but I think its liberal Democrats that are overstepping the boundaries of the Constitution and are trying to rewrite it. Why do I believe it's the Democrats and not both parties? The liberal Democrats are the ones who have passed all the laws, which have allowed the federal government to intrude into our society. An example of liberal Democrats attempting to rewrite our Constitution is with the First Amendment. Where does it say that religious prayer cannot be said in schools? The First Amendment says this: "Congress shall make no law respecting an establishment of religion or prohibiting the free exercise thereof; or abridging the freedom of speech, or of the press; or the right of people peaceably to assemble, and to petition the Government for a redress of grievances."[11]

Liberals take the statement of respecting an establishment out of context and got laws passed to stop school prayer. When all they really had to do was pass a law for a moment of silence, in our schools, before class started. Since this moment of silence could be used for anything, some students might have chosen to pray to the God of their choice, but this could not be allowed. In my opinion, they passed a law that would not allow universal prayer. The establishment of a religion means just that. Our forefathers didn't want our federal government to form a religion and make it mandatory to follow that faith, as it was in England and is now in China.

The liberal Democrats, however, did get around this, by forcing our schools to teach the religion of Darwinism. The religion of Darwinism should have been stated as a theory, which it has always been, not as fact. Why is it a theory and not fact? Is there any scientific evidence to support it as fact? No, but it does teach that there isn't a God. By teaching the religion of Darwinism you can, in a sneaky way, get people to question the existence of a creator. In other words, we just happened to be some kind of mistake that just happened.

If you can wipe out the existence of a creator, then you can wipe out absolutes, and by wiping out absolutes you can wipe out what is right and what is wrong. One other statement to mention about Darwinism and the reason it is a religion. All religions are based on faith, even Atheism, and since there is no scientific evidence to support them in any way, it takes faith to believe in Darwinism and Atheism. Therefore Atheism and Darwinism are religions. You still might be wondering how Atheism is a religion. You have to have the belief that there isn't a God. Since you can't disprove the existence of God, it takes faith to believe that there isn't a God, which in itself makes it a religion.

Some people also believe that for Atheism to be a religion there has to be a deity involved. The deity in Atheism is man. How's that? Man replaces the God of other religions. Man is accountable to himself and no one else, while the Christian religion and some other religions, says that man is accountable to a god.

When people are asked about God, they are asked, "How strong is your faith?" and not "How strong is your religion?" When people who believe in Atheism are asked, "How do you know there isn't a God?" their reply is, "I just believe it." When you ask Darwinists for scientific proof, they give you examples, such as a cow has the same stomach as a whale, therefore a cow evolved from a whale. Human beings have the same internal organs as pigs. Maybe we should re-evaluate our existence? We might have evolved from pigs.

King Barack Obama

Chapter 19

Julius Caesar was known as the man who changed the Roman Republic to the Roman Empire. He seized power and became the dictator of Rome. Franklin Delano Roosevelt, was he the man who changed the United States from a republic to a democracy? I'm not sure if it was him, but somewhere from his presidency until Barack Obama's presidency, we lost our republic.

We are now about to lose our democracy. The only question is: will it be with thunderous applause? Will King Barack Obama be known as the man who changed the United States from a democracy to a communist nation? I believe that the KBO, with the aid of the Democratic Party, which has control of Congress, will at first change the federal government of the United States from a democracy to a socialistic nation. Then through federal government programs and political maneuvering, he will maneuver the United States into a full-blown communist nation, with him in charge.

The question that I have is: When Barack Obama turns our country into a communist nation; will it be like China or Russia? The Chinese people, they get to come and go as they please. There seems to be very little oppression by their centralized government. The Chinese people can leave their country; they can go on vacation anywhere in the world or within their country's borders, without getting special permission from their centralized government. They have all the freedoms we used to have. The only thing they can't do is vote for their next corrupt government leader, like we can.

Russia, on the other hand, was very oppressive. They wouldn't allow their people to leave their country. They told their people where they had to work. They were intrusive in their people's everyday lives. I believe our federal government will follow the path of Russia's style of communism. Our centralized federal government will be very oppressive. They will intrude into our everyday lives, forcing us to do whatever they tell us to do. The federal government enforcement agents will come and knock on our house or apartment doors, if we step out of line.

If you don't want to live in a Communist nation, then you better leave and live somewhere else, before the United States government orders the closing of all ports of exits and refuses to let you leave. The KBO only has four years, maybe eight to achieve this, depending on how much apathy the people of the United States have, so he will have to move rapidly before some of us wake up. I myself don't quite understand how someone would rather live under a tyrant than that of a free system of government.

Who are the tyrants in our country? Nancy Pelosi is one. Harry Reed, I think he's too much of a wimp to be a tyrant, so he must be at the beck and call of Nancy Pelosi. How's Nancy Pelosi a tyrant? Tyrants oppress all forms of opposition. If you're opposed to her ideas, then through her power as Speaker of the House you are censored. Not one Republican had a say in that pork barrel spending bill that was passed by Congress.

The KBO has the potential to be a tyrant. He's already told people not to listen to Rush Limbaugh. He has stepped beyond his authority as President of the United States and fired the CEO of General Motors. He has demanded that contracts, AIG had with their executives be null and void. The KBO wants the fairness doctrine reinstated to oppress freedom of speech, but he excludes organizations that agree with him, like the lackeys of the Democratic Party news media.

Will the people of the United States wake up before it's too late? Some will, but I think most of the people of the United States will not. They don't think or understand what kind of bondage awaits them. The people of the United States are also slow to act or react. Sometimes we don't act at all, we just go about our business, not caring what happens to our nation. The reason some of us never react is because more and more of us have been conditioned, by our federal government-controlled school system. To believe that we can't take care of ourselves or we are too stupid to do so. So we will enjoy getting whatever we want from our federal government before they take it away.

The country of Germany after WWI was set up as a democracy. Germany, which lost the war, had to pay restitution for the war. The amount of money was so severe that the Germans couldn't pay it. Hyperinflation and economic hard times fell on Germany. The German mark was basically worthless. This aided Adolf Hitler in his attempt, to rise to a position of power and change the government, in Germany to Fascism. Hitler was revered as a messiah, he was going to restore Germany and bring prosperity back with his leadership. Be careful of people you raise to the level of messiah.

When Germany had free elections, Hitler ran for public office and got 30% of the vote. At least the people of Germany had more sense then we have today. They could see how bad a tyrant he would be. Although the German people didn't want him at first, Hitler used a series of events, which Germany was going through to his advantage. With the aid of economic hard times, which the German people were experiencing, he managed to force his way up to seize power in Germany after Hindenburg died.

Hitler became the dictator of Germany. The question I have is: Are we seeing the same type of power grab from the Democratic Party? I believe we are. Democrats are trying to oppress all opposition to their form of government takeover. One way of doing this is by stopping freedom of speech. Another way is to tell lies until every person in the United States believes them. Hitler was a master at this, so are liberal politicians. One lie is that our economy is the worst since the Great Depression. It's not true, but it will be soon, under their leadership. The next question is: Are we the people of the United States going to allow our freedoms to be taken away by these Marxist Democrats?

It's funny, when a country has an economic downturn. Some people have to blame someone else for their problems. In the case of Germany, it was the Jews. Although our problems stem from the brainless politicians, we have running the federal government. Democrats are blaming the rich cats in business. Be careful. We get our jobs from these rich cats in business.

What should we do with these brain-dead politicians? Vote them out of office. Voting them out of office is our only chance. The people we elect in their place have to understand that we want them to start paying off our national debt and govern under a balanced budget. If the ones we voted in don't follow our guidelines, then we vote them out of office too, but we don't replace them with the same old typical politicians. We need true change, not the KBO type of change.

Germany had hard times in their country, brought on by the peace treaty of Versailles, which led to the outbreak of WWII. Germany wanted revenge. We will have hard times, brought on by the pork barrel spending law of the KBO and Nancy Pelosi. How will this bring economic hard times to our country? Most of the money spent under this law, will be by wasteful federal government and state government programs. This bill was not passed by our elected officials, in the federal government, to create jobs; it was done to gain power over us. If you want to stimulate the economy, you need to create more disposable income and give that to the people. How's this for an example? Give $25,000 a year for the next four years to every legal working citizen of the United States. They must abide by two rules: they can only save half of it. The other half, they have to spend. This will stimulate the economy, plus the banks won't leave that money lying around, they will put it out into the economy in the form of investments and loans.

The KBO has stated that we can hold his administration accountable. How can we do that besides voting him out of office after his first term? Four years can be a long time when someone is out to destroy your country. If we can hold his administration accountable, can we tell him to ask for the resignation of one of his cabinet members? Can we tell him to resign? He probably won't go along with that. Then can we hold a recall vote, to remove him from the office of the Presidency and replace him with a non-elitist? I haven't found that in the Constitution of the United States.

A recall vote has never been done before on a sitting President of the United States, but hopefully we have that right and can do a recall vote within the first term of his presidency. If the KBO shows any sign of dictatorship on his part, we should demand a recall vote and remove him from public office. The Democratic Party, which has control of Congress, will not impeach him, no matter what he does.

There have been two presidents who should have had a recall vote put on them, and then removed from office. One was Jimmy Carter and the other was Bill Clinton. There should have been a recall vote on Jimmy carter in his second year as president, while a recall vote should have been done to Bill Clinton in his second year of his second term as president. So why wasn't there? The people of the United States, on the most part, are patient people. We are slow to anger. So we will endure the embarrassment of a President like Bill Clinton. We will endure the financial hardships brought on by a President like Jimmy Carter.

Now in today's timeframe, I don't know if we will endure the economic hardships that the KBO will bring to our nation. I don't know if we have the people in this country who have the fortitude of the people in the 1930s. The KBO will bring on a worldwide depression, which will make the depression of the 1930s look like a mild recession. The world is also a different place today, than it was in the 1930s. People took care of themselves back then. Today we have people who want the world governments to take care of them.

Will there be a recall vote on Barack Obama? When the people of the United States have endured enough hardship from his presidency, they might demand a recall vote. I believe that once the people of the United States realize that this so-called stimulus package was designed to pay back favors, to the KBO supporters, they might get angry enough to act. This stimulus package, passed by our Congress, which is controlled by the Democratic Party, and signed by the KBO, has mortgaged our great-grandchildren's future. Will this be enough for the people of the United States to act? I can only hope.

So why am I so down on the KBO's stimulus package? It's named wrong. It should be called the law that mortgaged our great-grandchildren's future, so he could pay back favors to his supporters. This law will only stimulate more debt, not our economy. Can you spend money and not stimulate the economy? The answer is yes. For instance, if you spend more money on welfare, will you stimulate the economy? No, you won't. Economies are stimulated by spending money on something that needs to be replaced, which means someone will have to remake it. People on welfare have very little, if any, disposable income. They are given everything they need to live out a meager existence.

Will the people of the United States rebel and take it to the streets, if a recall vote is considered to be unconstitutional? If the hardship is too great and the people of the United States don't have an out, then yes, there will be street demonstrations. The people of the United States who lived through the Great Depression will have endured nothing, in comparison, to what the people of the United States will have to endure under the presidency of the KBO.

Tyrants and dictators have a way of showing up when there are economic hard times in countries. Who is going to show up, when economic hard times hits the world, which was brought on by the KBO's stimulus package? I do have a question that has been bothering me for quite some time: Could the Democratic Party, which hates the United States and Christians, be destroying our economy, to bring a new tyrant up into world politics, so he can seize power and form a one-world government?

Holding Barack Obama and His Administration Accountable

Barack Obama said we could hold him and his administration accountable. How can we do this? Considering that he and his administration can do far more damage to our society and country. Before we the people of the United States can hold him and his administration accountable, by voting them out of office. I think that we should get a law passed that will hold him and his administration accountable today. By telling them, for every lie they tell, we get to pull a tooth out of their mouths. We'll be nice and start in the back part of their mouths and move forward. When we run out of teeth in their mouths, we will go to their significant other's mouths and start pulling their teeth. If he and his administrators continue with their lies, we go to their children's mouths. If this starts to work and they stop telling lies, then we can pass laws that will put the same penalty on our Congress members.

I know that none of our politicians would have any teeth within the first week of them taking office, but they might care for their significant other's teeth, and if not their significant other's teeth, they might care about their children's teeth.

I know, children can't be held accountable for the actions of their parents and spouses shouldn't be held accountable to the actions of their significant others. Unless they supported and aided in the lies their significant others tell.

If our servants don't care for anyone in their families, then we can just have fun seeing them go on TV trying to pronounce words without their teeth. One of the stipulations in the law would be no false teeth can be made, to replace teeth that have been pulled for lying to the people of the United States. I do think that this would be more of an incentive to them, to tell the truth, than any threat of jail time.

So why don't we do it? Trying to get laws passed to hold politicians accountable is nearly impossible, but it can't hurt to try. So the first thing we need to do is to call our congressional representatives. If that doesn't work, we need to get web sites started, saying we want this law passed in very simple language that a first-grader could understand. I know most of our politicians aren't as smart as first-graders.

So it should be written something like this: If a politician and/or one of his administrators lie, they will have one tooth pulled for every lie they tell. Children are exempted from said punishment. Significant others that have aided in this lie will not be exempt. Teeth that are pulled because of lies told to the people of the United States cannot be replaced with false teeth.

Why do I think this would work, considering that jail time doesn't even faze them? Politicians are like models. They are aware of their appearance and know that they have to look good, to be able to hoodwink the public. We think good looking means a good and decent person. Can you imagine if a politician tried running for public office with half his teeth missing, and people knew that half his teeth were missing because of him telling lies? I think it might work, how about you?

Is Barack Obama the Herald for the Anti Christ?

I put this here even though I could have put this in chapter 17 under religion. I thought it was more appropriate here. I know what some people are thinking, that people have been looking for the Anti Christ to come onto the stage of existence, for quite some time. But I do think we are in the End of Days and I do take the Bible as the word of God. So that being said, is Barack Obama the herald for the Anti Christ? He might not know that he is, but it surely looks, as if, he is getting the world ready for a world leader to take power.

Although some people think Barack Obama is the Anti Christ that has been foretold in the Bible, in the Book of Revelation. Pastor John Hagee says he isn't. So could Barack Obama be the herald for the Anti Christ as John the Baptist was for Jesus Christ? The same questions were asked when Bill Clinton was President of the United States, and Clinton's wife added to that speculation. In my opinion, you would have to really look hard to find a woman who is as evil and as corrupt as Hilary Clinton.

Why would people look upon these two men as the Anti Christ or possibility the herald for the Anti Christ? All you have to do is look at their activities and see why some people would think that. They both hate the United States. I think Barack Obama hates the United States more than Bill Clinton does. When Bill Clinton was President, he tried to make himself appear, as if he was the world leader, not just the President of the United States, and now you are seeing the same from Barack Obama.

Why would questions like this be running around the Christian community? There are a lot of Christians who believe we are in the period called the End of Days, and for that to happen, the Anti Christ has to take power and form a one-world government. This hasn't happened yet, so anyone who comes close to what the Bible describes as the Anti Christ, Christians sit up and start, to take notes on the possibility that this one might be it.

So what are some of the mannerism that the Anti Christ will have? He will be a great deceiver. This matches Barack Obama. He will be a very charismatic person. This also matches Barack Obama. He will be worshiped as a messiah. There are people in the United States who do worship Barack Obama. He will be considered to be a peace-loving man who will bring wars that will wipe out a third of the world's population. This we will have to wait and see. He will come out of Europe. This doesn't fit Barack Obama.

So far, out of our history, the one that fits this description the most was Adolph Hitler. He was worshiped as a messiah by the German people. He rose to power out of Europe. Some people took his mark of the SS and joined his special group of mass murderers. The German people followed him into one of the bloodiest periods in human history. Hitler and his allies, in their war against the world, caused 50 million people to lose their lives, but this will be nothing compared to what is about to happen. When the Anti Christ does hit the scene, two billion people will lose their lives in a war. A seven-year peace treaty will be signed between Israel and the world, which will be broken after three-and-a-half years.

Why does the Anti Christ need a herald, as Jesus did with John the Baptist? The Anti Christ is supposed to mimic Jesus, and since Jesus had a herald, so will the Anti Christ. Some think that his herald will be the False Prophet, but I don't know. I think the False Prophet will be more like a disciple.

So the question keeps coming up: Is Barack Obama the herald for the Anti Christ? Let's look at what Barack Obama is doing. Barack Obama is trying to bankrupt the United States by running up debt. His debt will equal the debt that has been created from the first president of the United States to the forty-third president of the United States. He speaks to the world, as if, he is the ruler of the world. He is also worshipped as a messiah. It's nauseating to me, when I see one of these people that worship him. I wonder how this person has gone wrong and why he decided to worship a man instead of God.

When the United States is bankrupt by Barack Obama's policies and programs, will he try to throw our sovereignty to the United Nations? Then what would be the next job, for the herald of the Anti Christ? Will he then try to form a one-world religion for everyone to worship the Anti Christ under?

Appeasement: It Doesn't Work

Chapter 20

Our elected officials are supposed to do the will of the people and show that they want to protect our country through strength, not through appeasement. Appeasement doesn't work, but liberal Democrats have never seemed to learn this lesson. Joe Kennedy was a big supporter of appeasing Hitler before WWII. He got the rude awakening of appeasement. He realized that you couldn't appease a dictator after Hitler attacked Poland. Will we get this same rude awakening under the Barack Obama's administration?

Here's an attempt to appease the Muslims extremists in the world: A teacher in California forced her students to say prayers to Allah, to worship him as Muslims do and to praise Allah. When two boys refused to kneel, they were punished with detention. "Some parents tried to sue the school but the judge threw the case out."[5] A liberal judge named Phyllis Hamilton, appointed by Bill Clinton, was also on the side of appeasement. She totally disregarded our Constitution and ruled that separation of church and state doesn't apply when it comes to any religion other than Christianity.

What she was saying is that the First Amendment of our Constitution only applies when a liberal judge hears a case against Christianity. Other religions don't fall under the guidelines of the First Amendment. So these Christian students who look to praising Allah as worshiping a false god, had no rights as far as saying they weren't comfortable worshiping a false god. Whether you believe

Allah to be a false god or not, the First Amendment applies across the board, when it comes to separation of church and state.

It's funny about the anti-Christian liberal organizations. When they want to remove a Christian symbol, they scream bloody murder, saying that children were forced to see it or people will be offended if they are around it, but people being offended by other religious symbols are told to get over it. When the anti-Christian liberal organizations wanted the saying "under God" in the Pledge of Allegiance removed, they said that their children were forced to say it. Liberal organizations tell people who get offended by their push, to remove Christian religion symbols that they should have tolerance for other people's belief systems. Well, that's good, but liberals need to practice what they preach.

Appeasement at Any Cost

I wonder if liberal Democrats believe they can appease the terrorists and then we can go back to the way it was. Well, there are three names I like to use to discredit that philosophy, and they are Jimmy Carter, Bill Clinton and John Kerry.

Under President Carter, nothing was worth fighting for. People were running to night school to learn how to speak Russian, because we thought for sure that we would be under the control of the USSR. But Reagan was elected President in 1980 and changed Jimmy Carter's course of destruction. Instead, he caused the USSR to crumble and fall. Today, Russia is a democracy. For how long, I don't know.

Bill Clinton was the Neville Chamberlain of the years from 1993 to 2001, while Barack Obama will be the Neville Chamberlain of the years from 2009 to whenever he leaves office. Bill Clinton believed that the terrorist problem was a law enforcement problem. Now Barack Obama seems to have the same belief as Bill Clinton. I wonder if Bill Clinton thought as Barack Obama thinks today, that he can reason with these world terrorists. John Kerry also thinks the terrorist problem, we are facing today, is a law enforcement problem.

I believe that a majority of Democrats believe this way. Two questions: Is it better to stop an attack, or let it happen and then look for the person or persons responsible, and put them on trial for this crime against humanity? Is it better to stop a murder, or just let it happen and look for the person or persons that committed this crime? I think it would be better to stop this activity before it gets started. Most of the time in law enforcement, the crime happens, then the police are called in, to investigate the crime. They then look for the people or person responsible for the crime. This is reactive not proactive work. So which one is better? To the one who was murdered, proactive work would have been better. He would still be alive. To the 3,000 people murdered in the terrorist attacks and to their family members, I think proactive work would have been better. So when Barack Obama says that the terrorists were caught and put on trial for their actions, what he is saying is he doesn't care how many people get killed, as long as we caught the people responsible after the act.

Bill Clinton; was he the lackey to Saddam Hussein? He was very soft on terrorism, when push came to shove. So Bill Clinton for eight years did nothing or very little when it came to fighting terrorism, which gave the terrorists enough time to set up the global network they have today. Hopefully the Barack Obama Administration will not be a reprieve to the terrorists in the world, as WWII was a reprieve to the CCP in China.

We did have a president who was willing to take the fight to the terrorists, but now, we have the appeasers of our time that are thinking like Neville Chamberlain and Joe Kennedy, appease them at any cost. I guess we will never understand that appeasement doesn't work. These terrorists are like the bully of the school playgrounds. If you try to appease him, it only emboldens him more.

One example to look at, which shows that appeasement doesn't work, is wife beating. When a husband beats his wife and if she becomes more submissive to him, the beatings usually intensify. This must be part of human nature. If you feel you are going to get away with it, you do it more frequently.

The terrorists of the world only understand force. They feel that if you do nothing, then you must be afraid of them. Therefore you will do nothing, and they will get away with whatever they do. They won't receive any kind of punishment for their actions. To understand terrorism, you have to understand the mindset of these people. If they only understand force, then negotiations would only be used as a ploy to get world support, or to buy them some time to regroup.

The cost of appeasement to us was 3,000 lives in New York, Washington, and a field in Pennsylvania. If we the people of the United States allow these appeasers to go back to their law enforcement ideology, how many will die then? Since we are at war with terrorists, we will get hit again it just depends on how hard. Appeasing them will make the attacks more severe. Why's that? To appease them, we will leave them alone and try to get along with them, which will give them time to regroup and attack us with everything they have, instead of what they have left.

The Socialistic Liberal Democratic Party still can't get it through their thick skulls that appeasement doesn't work. When one nation tries to appease another nation, the nation that is being appeased, soon looks to the other nation as being weak, and then attacks them. This is proven throughout history. The most recent case is WWII. Germany and Japan were being appeased by the League of Nations, and we all know what happened. Germany attacked Poland while Japan attacked China and started WWII. We were brought into the war after Japan attacked Pearl Harbor.

I myself do not like war. I would like to live in peace with other human beings, but there are times when you have to fight and this is one of them. I just wish we wouldn't learn this the hard way every time. Pearl Harbor the first time, and the Twin Towers the second time, and now that we are getting tired of the war on terrorism, we think we can turn tail and run back to our country and everything will be okay. Well, you better think twice, because if you allow the appeasers to do this, we will be hit again and more than 3,000 will lose their lives.

A Plea to Bring Back Strong Family Values

Chapter 21

I plead with the people of the United States: We need to bring back the strong family values that we had back in the 1950s, which China still has today. China has more sense than to try to destroy their family structure, which is one of the core foundations of their society. This foundation started before the forming of the Xia Dynasty.

Although China has a one-child-per-family law in place, the Chinese still raise their children to be respectful to their elders and to respect other people's property. If we can bring back family values, we can then bring back the disciplining of our children, to where we can instill in them that they need to be respectful to their elders and to other people's property.

Every society has it exceptions, and China is no different from any other country. The exception you will see in China is to see spoiled children with bad manners. While the exception in the United States is to see children that are well behaved and have respect for other people's property.

So what happened to us? How did we let this happen to us? Why are bad mannered children the norm in the United States? The answer to this is liberalism. Liberalism has caused all this. We allowed liberal Democrats to infiltrate our family structure with their laws that looked good and seemed good, but in reality they were destructive to the family structure and to our society's core foundation.

When I say we have to get back to the family values of the 1950s, some people think that means only the father works. No, that's not what I mean. Women who want to pursue a career should go after their dreams. I don't believe when a woman pursues her dreams that it will screw up the family. In The Old Testament, Proverbs 31:10 describes a virtuous woman. She owns land, she works the land, then she sells the crop at the market and she provides for her family and maidens. This sounds to me like a very busy woman. For the women who want to stay at home and raise a family, that's fine too. I'm not saying that one is better than the other. I'm just trying to say that a woman can pursue her dreams as well as the man can.

Where women in the United States made their mistake is they have listened to the Fem-A-Nazis, who say that treating a man with respect and kindness, causes them to lose their independence. No, what that really causes is a divorce. By the way, marriage is not an independent thing. Marriage is two people working together, relying on one another. If you want independence, then don't get married, because your marriage won't last with that kind of attitude. The reason I married my wife is because she knew that marriage is not two independent people running around doing their own thing, but two people working together toward a common goal.

She realized that marriage is a two-way street, and if you want it to last, then you need to return the kindness, respect and love you receive. Do all women in the United States listen to the feminist group NOW? No, the ones who don't listen to NOW probably have lasting relationships with their husbands. If they're not married, they probably have a happy life with friends and relatives. They have a good nature about them with a smile on their face. It's funny, these women who call themselves feminists, very seldom do I see them smiling. It seems that they always have something to complain about.

If women working didn't screw up the family, then what has screwed up our families? I believe it is the federal government's intrusion into our lives. They got a foothold into our family lives by saying, "We care about your children," but they didn't stop there.

They forced their way into raising our children and putting laws into effect, which forced parents to stop disciplining their children. These laws were supposed to keep child abusers from abusing their children. What it has done, is it has stopped parents from disciplining their children by the threat of jail time, by the state governments and the federal government.

Why would parents be afraid to discipline their children? The child is assumed to be telling the truth and the parents are assumed to be lying, even when the parents are put into separate rooms and come up with the same details, of the events that happened. Children are still believed to be telling the truth, even when they are put into separate rooms and come up with two totally different stories.

So how many of our children are juvenile delinquents? We as a society didn't stop our federal government, and as usual we let them go too far. Now it might even be too late to stop them and reverse the course they have set for the destruction of the family, which will bring on the destruction of our country. When we allowed our federal government to infiltrate our lives, we lost freedoms and liberties.

When some of our politicians (not liberal politicians) realized they screwed up the family, they tried to do something about the situation regarding our children, but liberal Democrats got another ridiculous law passed, which put parents between a rock and a hard place. What the liberal Democrats got passed was a law that held the parents financially accountable for their children's destructive actions.

How did this put the parents between a rock and a hard place? Let's analyze this. Parents are not allowed to discipline their children by threat of jail time from government bureaucrats, but then the same government bureaucrats says that they are going to hold you financially responsible, for your children's destructive actions.

I am amazed at this. Am I the only one who can see how laughable this law is? First the federal government, which at that time was run by liberal Democrats, destroyed the family values through high taxes, and with laws that threaten parents with jail time, which made it impossible for them to discipline their children. To get children to behave, you sometime have to discipline them, to make them understand that the world is not fair, and that you can't just go through life doing whatever you want, at the expense of others.

What is going to stop children's destructive behavior if there is no threat of punishment for wrong behavior? What stops an adult's destructive behavior? The destructive behavior of an adult is stopped by the threat of punishment which for them is jail time or execution. This usually gives them an attitude adjustment. So if the threat of punishment works for adults, than it should work for children.

What should have been done to get the parents back as head of the household? How about passing laws that rewarded parenting, and tax cuts that would have allowed the parents to quit their part-time jobs, which means they could spend time with their children? But you see this would also mean that liberal Democrats would have to give up some of the power they hold over us. So instead of liberals doing the right thing, they passed more ridiculous laws, which cause us to pay even higher taxes.

What do I mean by strong family values? I mean a family with strong unity. Another way of putting it would be: They do things together and the parents are there to raise their children, to discipline them when necessary, and to guide them into becoming responsible adults when they grow up. What we need to do, is tell the school-teachers to teach and only stick their nose into a family's business, when there is true child abuse happening. These teachers have no business sticking the nose into the parents business, just because they not following the political correctness jargon set forth by liberal politicians, or because parents are disciplining their children.

Is the federal government totally to blame for the breakdown of the family? No, but I believe they are at least 80% responsible and the parents are 20% responsible. Some parents gave away the responsibility of raising their children. This is the 20% of the blame that falls into play. The 80% of blame that falls on our federal government is through the laws they have passed, and by growing the federal government, to be the tax burden it has become to the working men and women of the United States.

Taxes got so high that in some families, both parents have to work a full-time and part-time job. The result of this has taken parents' time away from raising their children. The parents are now too busy trying to be friends with their children, instead of being parents. This is another reason why parents don't discipline their children.

God spelled out how we should live as a family. God comes first, then your mate and then the children. Liberal Democrats have tried to eliminate God from the family and replace God with the federal government. When we allow liberals to do this, we got God's commandment on how to live as a family screwed up.

When we get the family screwed up, we get our morals screwed up. When we get the family and our morals screwed up, we get our nation screwed up. When we get our nation screwed up, we get our ideals screwed up, and lifestyle becomes more important than the security of our nation and the unity of the family. When we get our priorities screwed up, we allow corrupt people into public office, such as Bill Clinton and Barack Obama.

So how do we get back to a strong, unified family, such as a Chinese family? I believe we need to take back the children from the federal government. Nazi Germany tried this by taking children away from their parents. Some parents gave them willingly, and history has showed us the results. We need to take back our schools from the federal government. Then once again we can truly call them public schools. We can see what has happened to children who receive an education under the state's doctrine. History shows us this. All you have to do is review Nazi Germany's history and Russia's history.

How many parents can actually say they have a say in the education their children receive, or does our federal government by the Department of Education set the curriculum? Right now, it seems that the federal government schools are indoctrinating our children into a socialism way of thinking, which corrupts them into thinking that the federal government is their god. If they worship the federal government, then this god will solve all their problems. If they just sit back and listen and give 100% of their salaries in the form of taxes, everything will be all right.

A Plea to Bring Back the Traditional Family

The traditional family has come under attack lately by liberal organizations, which are quick to jump on the bandwagon, when occasionally one of the parents is a child abuser or an alcoholic. They are quick to point out, how bad, it is to the children who have to live under these conditions. I do believe this to be true, it is bad for children to have to live under these conditions. But it's funny to see how fast liberal politicians and liberal organizations come running to the defense of a non-traditional family. They say that the children of these types of families will suffer no adverse side effects.

If you talk to any child abuser, you will hear most of them say how much they love their children. Most alcoholics will say the same. A lot of them will fight the state's decision to take their children away. The situation with the child abuser, it's quite simple to see why a child will have emotional scars for the rest of his/her life. With the alcoholic, it could be a different story. Alcoholics, who love their children, provide them with a good home to live in and take care of them. He/she is not any worse of a parent than a homosexual or lesbian, at least on the surface.

Liberal Democrats are quick to point out studies that have been made, to show that a child living under the same roof as an alcoholic will suffer emotional scars. This is interesting. There are alcoholics that do provide for their families. The only thing is they can't stay away from the bottle. Does this cause the child, to have some kind of subconscious reaction to one of the parents? If so, then why wouldn't a child have the same kind of subconscious reaction to a perverse, deviant lifestyle, such as a homosexual or lesbian marriage?

I'm sure that these homosexuals and lesbians will tell you that they do love the children they adopt. So what's the problem? The problem is that a gay lifestyle falls outside the realm of normal, as does the child abuser and alcoholic. I believe that children will suffer emotional scars, when they are subjected to abnormal lifestyles. So why haven't we seen any homosexual and lesbian marriage studies, which show any adverse affect on children that live in that type of family? That's easy, we haven't been conducting any studies to see if there is any adverse affect on children, and it's also politically correct to turn a blind eye to this activity.

So when could we see any possible side effects from this type of abnormal lifestyle? When these children grow up and become adults is when we will see, if there is any adverse side affect to them, from the lifestyle they were raised in. Not all children raised in an abnormal lifestyle allow their emotional scars to influence them, in their adult life. In other words, they overcome their emotional scars and become productive members of our society

Do I believe God, when He said, "Here's how you have a successful marriage and family"? Do I believe the Bible, which is the word of God, which goes into greater detail on how to have a successful family and marriage? Yes, I do.

I Plead With the People of the United States

My plea to the people of the United States is this: We have to get involved in our country's politics. We have to care enough to take the time, to see what kind of person we are voting for, for public office. You are probably asking yourself, why? After all, politics turns my stomach. Yes, I know, liberal politicians with all their lying and half-truths turn my stomach, too, but you have to understand that this is what they are hoping for. A complacent society is what liberal Democrats love, because they know if you took the time to investigate them, you wouldn't vote for them, and you probably would vote them out of office. We need to get involved in politics. Why is this? Well, politics, whether you like it or not, decides what kind of life you will have.

You can choose a life with a big, bloated, slow-moving federal government looking over your shoulder. Pulling out your wallet, taking whatever amount of money is needed to run such a government. You can choose a federal government that is socialistic, which is intrusive in your life and passes laws that take away your freedoms and liberties.

You can turn a blind eye to what is happening to our country because your lifestyle is more important. You can be complacent and go about your merry way, but sooner or later, it will catch up to you. So how do we stop our course of destruction? By getting involved in politics, I don't mean that you should run for public office, but you should know what kind of man/woman you're voting for.

For instance, I knew what kind of man Bill Clinton was when he was running for president. I made sure I didn't vote for him. Some people I talked to, voted for him because he was a Democrat and that was good enough for them. Others told me that they were going to vote for Clinton because he was a good-looking man, and some I talked to, told me, they were going to vote for Clinton because his wife was better looking than his opponent's wife. Well, so much for voting for your convictions. I would rather see these types of people not vote than to aid in the destruction of our country, by voting for people who are politically motivated for their own personal and financial gratification.

I didn't vote for Barack Obama because he is one of the biggest phonies that the Democratic Party has managed to come up with. His gimmick of hope and change didn't fool me. I could see that his change was the same old worn-out policies that the Democratic Party has been trying for the last 40 years.

If it is part of human nature for countries to rise to power, only to fall from power after 20 years to 300 years, of being the big dog on the block. Then all we can hope to do is prolong our superpower position. We can do this by getting involved, by voting for people who have the best interest of the country in mind, not their own welfare or the welfare of their special interest groups. To clarify this, we as a nation have to decide what role our federal government should have in the history of our country. I, for one, am for a very limited role.

ENDNOTES:

Chapter 1:

[1] "Shocking Video Unearthed Democrats in the own words Covering up the Fannie Mae, Freddie Mac Scam that caused our Economic Crisis," YouTube - Shocking Video Unearthed Democrats in their own wo…, Congressional hearing late 2004, Naked Emperor News.com www.youtube.com/watch?v=_MGT_cSi7Rs

[2] "Timeline shows Bush, McCain warning Dems of financial and housing crisis; meltdown," YouTube – Timeline shows Bush, "McCain warning Dems of financ…, Fox news Channel Wednesday September 24, 2008. "Special report with Brit Hume." www.youtube.com/watch?v=cMnSp4qEXNM

[3] "How many babies are killed a day by abortion?" How many babies are killed a day by abortion? – Yahoo Answe… answers.yahoo.com/question/index?qid=20071117145… P.1

Chapter 3:

[1] "What was tax rate when colonies seceded from Britain," WikiAnswers – What was tax rate, when colonies seceded from B… wiki.answers.com/Q/What_was_tax_rate_when_coloni... P.1

[2] Susan Page, "Most Americans OK with Big Government, at least for now," USA TODAY, Updated 4/15/2009. www.usatoday.com/news/washington/2009-04-14-bigg... P.1

[3], [4] Wealthcare, "the Tax Poem," LawNews.TV Blog, August 14, 2008 lawnews.tv/blog/2008/08/14/the tax poem/ P.4, P.5

Chapter 4:

[1] Stanley K. Schultz, Professor of History, William P. Tishler, Producer, "H102Lecture 27: The Almost Great Society: The 1960s," us.history.wisc.edu/hist102/lectures/lecture27.h... P.2

[2], [3] Steve Sailer UPI, "Black Illegitimacy Rate Declines" Black Illegitimacy Rate Declines others' Rise June 27, 2003. www.isteve.com/2003_black_illegitimacy_rate_decl... P.2, P3

[4] Robert E. Rector, "The Size and Scope Of Means-Tested Welfare Spending," The heritage Foundation, August 1, 2001 www.**heritage.org**/Research/Welfare/Test080101.cfm P.3

[5], [6] "THE 2009 HHS POVERTY GUIDELINES One Version of the [U.S.] Federal Poverty Measure," United States Department of Health & Human Services Jan 23, 2009. 2009 Federal **Poverty** Guidelines, **aspe.hhs.gov/poverty**/09**poverty**.shtml P.1

[7] Gordon M. Fisher, "Poverty Guidelines for 1992," Published in: Social Security Bulletin, Vol. 55, no. 1, Spring 1992, pp. 43-46, United States Department of Health & Human Services Aug 31, 2005. **Poverty Guidelines** [Background Paper] aspe.hhs.gov/poverty/papers/background-paper92.s... P.3

Chapter 8:

[1] "The Two Kingdoms (920-597)" JEWISH VIRTUAL LIBERAL, a division of the American-Israel Cooperation Enterprise www.**jewishvirtuallibrary.org**/jsource/History/**Kingdoms**1.html P.1

[2], [3], and [4] Shira Schoenberg, "Solomon," JEWISH VIRTUAL LIBERAL, a division of the American-Israel Cooperation Enterprise www.jewishvirtuallibrary.org/jsource/biography/S... P.2

<u>Chapter 10:</u>

[1] "Neolithic China," Dynasties of Ancient China www.**mnsu.edu**/emuseum/prehistory/**China**/ancient_**China**/**neolithic**.html P.1

[2] "Qi of Xia," <u>**Qi of Xia** - Wikipedia, the free encyclopedia</u>, en.wikipedia.org/wiki/Qi_of_Xia P.1

[3] "XIA DYNASTY" <u>**Xia Dynasty** - New World Encyclopedia</u> www.**newworldencyclopedia.org**/entry/**Xia_Dynasty** P.3

[4], [5] "Xia Dynasty" Xia Dynasty of Ancient China <u>**Xia**</u> www.mnsu.edu/emuseum/prehistory/China/ancient_ch... P.1

[6] Carl Limbacher and NewsMax.com Staff For the story behind the story…, "book: Hillary Used 'etiquette Squads' to Bust up Protests" Aug 26, 2002 America's news page – News Archives, additional archives inside cover, **archive.newsmax**.com/ P.1

[7] N.S. Gill, about.com "Xia Dynasty" <u>**Xia Dynasty** of Ancient China - **Xia Dynasty**</u> ancienthistory.about.com/od/Chinadynasties/p/032... P.2

[8] <u>Legends: **Jie** the Tyrant</u> 66.111.36.90/pages/culture/legends/**jie**.html P.1

[9], [10] Li Ung Bing Edited by Joseph Whiteside, "outlines of Early China History" 3.2. "Jie and Mei Xi" <u>Romance of Three Kingdoms - by Luo Guanzhong - History</u> threekingdoms.com/history.htm P.1, P.7

[11] <u>**Xia** Dynasty (2205-1806 BC)</u> www.**yutopian.com**/history/**xia**.html P.2

[12] **Shang** Dynasty ••(1783-1134 B.C.) www.yutopian.com/history/shang.html P.1

Chapter 11:

[1] "Shang Dynasty" Shang Dynasty of Ancient China **Shang** www.mnsu.edu/emuseum/prehistory/China/ancient_ch... P. 1

[2] Richard Hines "Ancient China: The Shang Dynasty 1766-1050 BC" updated June 06, 1999 Copyright 1996 Richard Hooker **Ancient China: The Shang, 1766-1050 BC** wsu.edu/~dee/ANCCHINA/SHANG.HTM P.1

[3], [4], [5], [6] Da Ji www.wku.edu/~yuanh/China/tales/daji_b.htm P.1, P.2

[7], [9], [10], [13], [14], [15], [16] "Zhou Dynasty" Zhou Dynasties of Ancient China **Zhou** www.mnsu.edu/emuseum/prehistory/China/ancient_ch... P.1

[8], Eastern Zhou (771 - 256 **BC) Spring & Autumn Peri...** www.umd.umich.edu/mitten/jsanteiu/Student%20Work/Chinese%2... P.1

[11], [12] "A Legend about Beacon Tower," Great Wall Apr 6, 2008 A Legend about Beacon Tower www.Chinatour360.com/greatwall/legend/beacon.htm P.1, P.2

Chapter 12:

[1] US Foreign Policy Encyclopedia "Protectorates and Spheres of Influence" **Protectorates and Spheres of Influence**: Information from Ans... www.answers.com/topic/protectorates-and-spheres-... P.5

[2] "Opium Wars" Anglo-**Chinese Wars** - Hutchinson encyclopedia article about A... encyclopedia.farlex.com/Anglo-Chinese+Wars P.1

[3] **Jonathan D. Spence,** "Sun Yat-sen" Aug 30, 1999. TIMEasia.com | **TIME 100**: **Sun Yat**-**sen** | 8/23/99-8/30/99 www.**time.com**/time/asia/asia/magazine/1999/990823/**sun_yat**_sen1.html P.3

[4] Who 2 Biography: "Chiang Kai-shek, Military / political Figure / World War II" **Chiang Kai-shek**: Biography from Answers.com www.**answers.com**/topic/**chiang-kai-shek** P.1

[5] ShortNews.com "**Teacher** Forces **Students** to Muslim **Prayer**" June 02, 2004 **Teacher** Forces **Students** to Muslim **Prayer** www.shortnews.com/start.cfm?id=39967 "Same Judge OK'ed Muslim Prayer" June 1, 2004. Source: www.newsmax.com P.1

Chapter 13:

[1], [2] "white Lotus Rebellion" White Lotus Rebellion — **Infoplease.com** www.infoplease.com/ce6/history/A0852123.html P.1

[3], [4] "Taiping Rebellion" Nov 5, 2008 New World Encyclopedia Taiping Rebellion - New World Encyclopedia www.newworldencyclopedia.org/entry/Taiping_Rebel P.1

[5], [7] Ch'ing China: The **Taiping** Rebellion For information contact: Richard Hines Updated 7-14-1999 Copyright 1996 Richard Hooker wsu.edu/~dee/CHING/TAIPING.HTM - 12k P.1

[6] Matthew Seiler, "Taiping Rebellion: the destruction of the Chinese culture," December 15, 1867 **Taiping Rebellion**: The destruction of the Chinese culture sun.menloschool.org/~sportman/westernstudies/sec... P.1

[8], [10], [11] Philip V. Allingham, "The Opium Trade, Seventh through Nineteenth Centuries" The Victorian Web Jun 24, 2006 England and China: The **Opium Wars**, 1839-60 www.victorianweb.org/history/empire/opiumwars/op... p.1, p.3

[9] "History > Shanghai's Multicultural History 1854-1949" Favenger Tethered Histories > Shanghai's Multicultural History 1854-1... www.favenger.org/pages/shanghai.html P.1

[12] Madeleine Lynn "THE STORY OF THE THREE KINGDOMS" Discover Yangtze.com, THE STORY OF THE THREE KINGDOMS www.discoveryangtze.com/Yangtzediscovery/the_sto... P.1

[13] "Russian Academic U.s Downfall, Interesting, discuss?" Runescape Community Dec 30, 2008 Russian Academic Predicts U.s Downfall - Runescape Community www.zybez.net/community/index.php?showtopic=1170... P.1

[14] "Western Han" Travel China Guide.com China **Western Han** Dynasty: Emperors, Politics, Economy, Cult... www.travelChinaguide.com/intro/history/han/weste... P.1

[15], [16], [17] Jonathan Wu "Wang Mang Ruled (AD 8-22 BC) Han Ruler and Emperor Biographies **Wang Mang** - Xin Ruler and Emperor Biographies - English kongming.net/novel/han/wangmang.php P.1

Chapter 14:

[1], [2], [3], [4] Filed by Jim Lakely on March 15, 2009 "Judge orders Christian parent to stop home schooling her kids" The American Culture, The American Culture: **Judge** orders Christian parent to **stop** ... stkarnick.com/blog2/2009/03/judge_orders_christi... P.2

[5] N.S. Gill, "Fall of Rome – Reasons for the Fall of Rome Include the Economy and Hoarding," "Economic Reasons for the Fall of Rome" Economic Reasons for Why Rome Fell ancienthistory.about.com/cs/romefallarticles/a/f... P.1

[6], [7], [8], [9], [10] **Julian Fenner,** "To what extent were economic factors to blame for the deterioration of the Roman Empire in the Third Century A.D?" Economic Deterioration of Rome in the Third

Century AD by www.roman-empire.net/articles/article-018.html P.5

Chapter 15:

[1] **United States Unemployment** data www.nidataplus.com/lfeus1.htm P.2

[2], [3] US **unemployment rate** reaches 5.5% // **Current** current.com/items/89005335_us-unemployment-rate-… P.2

[4] Taxes – Bill Clinton vs. George Bush – Locker Room www.faniq.com/poll/Taxes—Bill-Clinton-vs-George... P.1

[5] How **many** babies are killed a **day** by **abortion**? – Yahoo! Answe… The Alan Guttmacher Institute. www.agi-usa.org. answers.yahoo.com/question/index?qid=20071117145… P.1

[6], [7], [8], [9], [10], [11], [12], [13], [14], [15], [16], [17], [18], [19], [20] **Al Mudhill,** "$ 338.3 BILLION DOLLARS A YEAR. Are we THAT stupid?" www.heartlandoutdoorsman.com/phpBB2/viewtopic.ph... P.1 & P.2

[21] **Vandals** www.sfusd.k12.ca.us/schwww/sch618/RomanLinks/Van... P.2

[22] Alaric the **Visigoth** Globusz Publishing www.globusz.com/ebooks/FamousMen/00000014.htm P.1

[23], [24], [25] History of the **Vandals** www.**roman-empire.net**/articles/article-016.html P.1

Chapter 16:

[1], [4], [5] "American Victims KILLED DURING mostly 'Palestinian' Arab TERRORIST ATTACKS" **AMERICAN**

VICTIMS KILLED DURING ARAB TERRORIST ATTACKS avpv.tripod.com/AmericanVictims.html P.1, P.3

[2] "Who murdered the athletes of the Israeli 1972 Olympic Team in Munich?" PALESTINE FACTS, ISRAEL 1967 – 1991 OLYPIC TEAM MURDER, Israeli 1972 Olympic Team Murdered in Munich www.palestinefacts.org/pf_1967to1991_munich.php P.1

[3], [7], [8], [9], [10] "CHRONOLOGY OF MAJOR TERRORIST ATTACKS AGINST U.S. TARGETS," CDI TERRORISM PROJECT **Terrorism - Terrorist** Attacks **Chronology** Christopher Hellman, CDI Senior Analyst, chellman@cdi.org Victoria Garcia, CDI Research Assistant, vgarcia@cdi.org www.cdi.org/terrorism/chronology-pr.cfm P.3, P4

[6] Mitchell Bard, "Terror Aboard the Achille Lauro," JEWISH VIRTUAL LIBERARY A Division of The American – Israeli Cooperative Enterprise **Terror** Aboard the **Achille Lauro** eightiesclub.tripod.com/id301.htm P.1

[11], [12], [13] "Terrorist Attacks," (within the United States or against Americans abroad) Terrorist Attacks — **Infoplease**.com www.infoplease.com/ipa/A0001454.html P.1, P.2

[14] "Terrorism," RANDOM HOUSE WEBSTER'S COLLEGE DICTIONARY P.1329

[15] "Guerrilla warfare," RANDOM HOUSE WEBSTER'S COLLEGE DICTIONARY P.577

Chapter 17:

[1], [2] Mike White, "The War on Christians in American Public Schools" AC ASSOCIATED CONTENT, JULY O6, 2006 The War on **Christians** in American Public Schools - Associate... www.associatedcontent.com/article/41959/the_war_... P.2

[3] Truth Wins Out - **Focus on the Family** Daily Newsletter Consum... Posted September 10th, 2008 by Michael Airhart www.truthwinsout.org/blog/focus-on-the-family-da...

[4] "John 14:6" King James version of the Bible. Copyright (c) 1989 year by THOMAS NELSON PUBLISHERS

Chapter 18:

[1] Website: TeamGOP.com News Archive – March 2002, Article orientated in the FOXNEWS.COM HOME > POLITICS, Article's Title "Independent Prosecutor had Enough to Prosecute Clinton", dated March 6, 2002

[2] Website: Tom Daschle Tax problem Emerges: UPDATED, Article orientated in THE HUFFINGTON POST dated January 30, 2009, **UPDATE: February 3, 1:05PM ET: Additional reporting by Sam Stein and Rachel Weiner P.2**

[3] Website: Armstrong Williams: Tom Daschle: revving up for 2004 run, Article oriented in the Townhall.com, Where Your Opinion Counts, Dated January 16, 2002 By Armstrong Williams P.1

[4] Tax Foundation, "Distribution of the Federal Individual Income Tax," *Special Report* No. 101, November 2000.

[5], [6], [7] Daniel J. Mitchell, "The Truth About Tax Rates and The Politics of Class Warfare", Heritage Foundation, March 5, 2001. The Truth About **Tax** Rates and The Politics of Class Warfare www.heritage.org/Research/Taxes/BG1415.cfm P.1

[8], [9] "liberal," RANDOM HOUSE WEBSTER'S COLLEGE DICTIONARY P.756

[10] Robert S. McIntyre, "voodoo Economics: the sequel," "From the GOP Witch Doctors Who Busted the Budget, More Tax Cut Sorcery" The Washington Post OUTLOOK Sunday 25, 1994 CTJ

Editorial on Voodoo Economics by Robert McIntyre www.ctj.org/html/voodoo.htm P.3

[11] "FIRST AMENDMENT – RELIGION AND EXPRESSION" U.S. Constitution: First Amendment, Findlaw FOR LEGAL PROFESSIONALS FindLaw: U.S. Constitution: **First Amendment** caselaw.findlaw.com/data/constitution/amendment0... P.1

Other Sources/Suggestions for Reading

Social Security Online – History www.ssa.gov/history/35 actinx.html
Social Security Act of 1935 www.nationalcenter.org/SocialSecurityAct.html
Dick Morris and Eileen McGann, "The Dark Side of Hillary Clinton's Health Care Plan," REAL CLEAR POLITICS, September 22, 2007
www.realclearpolitics.com/articles/2007/09/the_d... - 25k -
Online NewsHour: "The healthcare Debate following Clinton's Healthcare Address to Congress," "A Detailed Timeline of the Healthcare Debate portrayed in "The System" Events following Clinton's healthcare Address to Congress through March 1994"
www.pbs.org/newshour/forum/may96/background/heal... **Federal Minimum Wage** Rates, 1955–2009 — Infoplease.com www.infoplease.com/ipa/A0774473.html
Social Security Act of 1935 www.nationalcenter.org/SocialSecurityAct.html
Great Society: Definition from Answers.com www.answers.com/topic/great-society
Emancipation Proclamation By the President: ABRAHAM LINCOLN
WILLIAM H. SEWARD, Secretary of State www.nps.gov/ncro/anti/emancipation.html
Xia Dynasty www.**Chinaculture.org**/gb/en_aboutChina/2003-09/24/content_22684.htm

China **Xia Dynasty** (21st-16th century BC), Slavery Society Hi... www.travelChinaguide.com/intro/history/xia

Carl Limbacher and NewsMax.com Staff For the story behind the story…, "More St. Pat's Day Intimidation by Hillary's Bodyguards" March 29, 2000 NewsMax.com: America's news page – News Archives, additional archives inside cover, ***archive.newsmax***.*com/*

Carl Limbacher and NewsMax.com Staff For the story behind the story…, "Hillary's Secret Service Agents Rough Up Reporters at St. Pat's Crowd Boos" March 17, 2000 America's news page – News Archives, additional archives inside cover, ***archive.newsmax***.*com/*

Chinese mythology: Information from Answers.com www.**answers.com**/topic/chinese-mythology

History of China www.**crystalinks.com**/Chinahistory.html

Chinese History - **Xia** and Shang **Dynasties** www.megaloceros.net/hist5.htm

Jie of **Xia** - Wikipedia, the free encyclopedia en.wikipedia.org/wiki/Jie_of_Xia

Chinese history - The **Xia Dynasty** (2070-1600 BC) www.Chinavoc.com/history/xia.htm

China **Xia Dynasty** (21st-16th century BC), Slavery Society Hi... www.travelChinaguide.com/intro/history/xia

Shang Dynasty **ancienthistory.about.com**/od/China/g/**ShangDynasty**.htm

Shang Dynasty (16th-11th century BC) www.**warriortours.com**/intro/history/**shang**

Shang Dynasty - MSN Encarta **encarta.msn.com**/encyclopedia_681500371/**Shang_Dynasty**.html

Shang Dynasty **polaris.gseis.ucla.edu**/yanglu/ECC_HISTORY_**SHANG DYNASTY**.htm

Chinese history - The **Shang Dynasty** (1600-1046 BC) www.Chinavoc.com/history/shang.htm

Shang Dynasty (16th -11th century BC), China History www.**travelChinaguide.com**/intro/history/**shang**

Shang Dynasty - New World Encyclopedia www.**newworldencyclopedia.org**/entry/**Shang_Dynasty**

SHANG DYNASTY members.tripod.com/~jonbyrdjonbyrd/shang.html

N.S. Gill, "Shang Dynasty" **Shang Dynasty** of Ancient China - **Shang Dynasty** ancienthistory.about.com/od/Chinadynasties/p/032...

King Zhou of Shang - Wikipedia, the free encyclopedia **en.wikipedia.org**/wiki/**King_Zhou_of_Shang**

Shang Dynasty - Wikipedia, the free encyclopedia en.wikipedia.org/wiki/Shang_Dynasty - 111k

Shang Dynasty **mysite.verizon.net**/vzerkqhk/minnuto/id23.html

Shang and **Zhou** Dynasties: The Bronze Age of China | Heilbrun... www.metmuseum.org/toah/hd/shzh/hd_shzh.htm - 37k

Di **Xin** encyclopedia topics | Reference.com www.**reference.com**/browse/Di+**Xin**?jss=0

Spring and **Autumn Period** - New World Encyclopedia www.**newworldencyclopedia.org**/entry/**Spring**_and_**Autumn_Period**

Chinese history - **Spring** & **Autumn Period** (722-481 BC) / Warring States **...** www.**Chinavoc.com**/history/**spring**and**autumn**.htm

The **Warring** States **Period** of Ancient China www.sjsu.edu/faculty/watkins/warringstates.htm

King You of Zhou - Wikipedia, the free encyclopedia **en.wikipedia.org**/wiki/**King_You_of_Zhou**

Zhou Dynasty: Definition from Answers.com www.**answers.com**/topic/**zhou**-dynasty-1

Baosi - Wikipedia, the free encyclopedia en.wikipedia.org/wiki/Baosi - 21k

Spring and **Autumn Period**: Information from Answers.com www.**answers.com**/topic/**spring**-and-**autumn**-**period**

Chinese history - **Spring** & **Autumn Period** (722-481 BC) / Warring States **...** www.**Chinavoc.com**/history/**spring**and**autumn**.htm

Schoolboys punished with detention for refusing to kneel dow... www.dailymail.co.uk/news/article-1031784/Schoolboys-punish...

Judge rules Islamic **education**
OK in California classroom... www.worldnetdaily.com/news/article.asp?ARTICLE_I...

List of judicial appointments made by **Bill Clinton**... en.wikipedia.org/wiki/List_of_judicial_ap...
The **Warring** States **Period** of Ancient China www.sjsu.edu/faculty/watkins/warringstates.htm
Qing Dynasty www.**mnsu.edu**/emuseum/prehistory/China/later_imperial_China/**qing**.html
Qing Dynasty - New World Encyclopedia www.**newworldencyclopedia.org**/entry/**Qing**_Dynasty
Ch'ing: Definition from Answers.com www.**answers.com**/topic/**qing**
History of Chinese **Qing** Dynasty (1644-1911), Manchu, Emperors www.**travelChinaguide.com**/intro/history/**qing**.htm
Qing Dynasty - MSN Encarta **encarta.msn.com**/encnet/refpages/RefArticle.aspx?refid=761557160
Qing Dynasty www.**Chinatour360.com**/history/**qing**-dynasty
Qing Dynasty - Wikipedia, the free encyclopedia **en.wikipedia.org**/wiki/**Qing**_Dynasty
Western Powers, Japan and Opium **in China** as **the Qing Dynasty** Goes into **...** **associatedcontent.com/.../western_powers**_japan_and_opium_**in_China**.html
Boxer Uprising 1900 www.**thecorner.org**/hist/**China**/boxer.htm
88. **Qing Dynasty** (En) www.**warriortours.com**/intro/history/**qing**/index.htm
Warlord Period www.ccds.charlotte.nc.us/touma/new_page_40.htm
Early Republic and **Warlord** Period www.thecorner.org/hists/China/warlords.htm
China, led by **Sun Yat Sen** www.**humanistictexts.org/sun_yat**.htm
Sun, Yat-sen www.**newworldencyclopedia.org**/entry/**Sun_Yat-sen**
Sun Yat-sen: Biography from Answers.com www.**humanistictexts.org/sun_yat**.htm
Sun Yat-sen's - Wikipedia, the free encyclopedia **en.wikipedia.org**/wiki/**Sun_Yat**
warlord: Definition from Answers.com www.**answers.com**/topic/**warlord**

Taiping Rebellion www.lycos.com/info/taiping-rebellion.html
As if Things Weren't Bad Enough, **Russian Professor Predicts** ... online.wsj.com/article/SB123051100709638419.html
Biggest **reasons** for the **fall** of **Rome**? - Yahoo! Answers answers. yahoo.com/question/index?qid=20081130084...
The Economic History of **the Western Roman Empire**: The Invasi... www.sjsu.edu/faculty/watkins/barbarians.htm
The Fall of **the Western Roman Empire**@Everything2.com everything2.com/title/The%2520Fall%2520of%2520th...
Alaric Trashes Rome — **410 AD** www.mmdtkw.org/VAlaric.html
The **Sack of Rome** penelope.uchicago. edu/~grout/encyclopaedia_roman...
BBC - History - **Rome's** Greatest Enemies Gallery www.bbc. co.uk/history/ancient/romans/enemiesrome...
Sack of Rome (Europe [**410**]) — Britannica Online Encyclopedi... www.britannica.com/EBchecked/topic/508876/Sack-o...
Vandals www.sfusd.k12.ca.us/schwww/sch618/RomanLinks/Van...
Brian Adam, "History of the Vandals" History of the **Vandals** www.roman-empire.net/articles/article-016.html
N.S. Gill, "Fall of Rome - Why Did Rome Fall" **Fall of Rome** - **Why Did Rome Fall** ancienthistory.about. com/cs/romefallarticles/a/f...
Hadrians Wall, extent of **the Roman Empire** https://edu-fs01.tgm. ac.at/dav/wolfgang.kugler.e1/pub...
Jake Jones, "NC Judge's decision threatens homeschoolers everywhere," examiner.com Evangelical Examiner: NC Judge's decision threatens homescho... www.examiner. com/x-2359-Evangelical-Examiner~y20...
washingtonpost.com: **Archive** www.washingtonpost. com/wp-dyn/nation/specials/attac...
John King Fairbank the Great Chinese Revolution P.1 – P.370
Conrad Schirokauer History of Chinese and Japanese Civilizations second edition P.3 – P.628
Bill O'Reilly TV. News hour
Census bureau
Hannity and Colmes TV news hour

LaVergne, TN USA
20 July 2010

190212LV00005B/178/P